Popular Communism:
Political Strategies and Social Histories in the Formation of the German, French, and Italian Communist Parties 1919-1948

by
Eric D. Weitz

Western Societies Program
Occasional Paper number 31
Cornell University
Ithaca, NY
1992

for Carol

Acknowledgements

Research support for this essay was provided by the National Endowment for the Humanities (NEH), the American Historical Association through its Bernadotte E. Schmitt Grant for Research in European, African or Asian History, and St. Olaf College. Aspects of the German section derive from research conducted in the former German Democratic Republic with the support of the International Research and Exchanges Board (IREX). I would like to thank all four institutions for their generous support. Both NEH and IREX operate with funds appropriated by the United States government. Neither the granting institutions nor the U.S. government are responsible for the views expressed in this essay.

I would also like to thank Geoff Eley, whose comments on a different paper prompted some of my efforts here, and Dolores Peters, who provided very helpful guidance through the French literature and debates. Hal Benenson, Gerd-Rainer Horn, Michel Le Gall, Norman Naimark, Dolores Peters, Sidney Tarrow, and the participants in the St. Olaf College Department of History Faculty Colloquium, the University of Minnesota Department of History Social History Workshop, and the University of Minnesota History and Society Program offered detailed and insightful comments on drafts of this paper. Earlier versions were read at the annual meetings of the Council for European Studies (1987) and the Social Science History Association (1989), and I would also like to thank the commentators at these sessions—Leonardo Paggi, Darryl Holter, and James Cronin—for their helpful criticism. Finally, I wish to express my appreciation to the reviewers for the Western Societies Program Occasional Papers Series.

Contents

Introduction

The revolutions of 1989-91 mark not only the collapse of communist regimes in central and eastern Europe and the Soviet Union. They also signal the end of the epoch of working-class political representation, the period defined by the emergence of mass socialist and communist parties that articulated a political philosophy centered on the proletariat as the agent of progress and social transformation and that had at their core working-class support. In its most vibrant phase, this epoch lasted from around the last decade of the nineteenth century through the 1950s, and its demise is not, of course, a new observation.[1] Socialist parties have long since shed their essential working-class character, and communist parties long ago lost the halo inscribed with the promise of human liberation. But with the breakdown of European communist regimes, the continual electoral decline of the French Communist Party, and the transformation of the Italian Communist Party into a democratic party of reform, the classic era of labor representation has at long last reached its terminus.

Within this epoch, and in the time span nearly coincident with the existence of the Communist International (1919-1943), four western European communist parties rose from isolated sects to mass-based, popular movements. In almost too neat a fashion, each of the parties under consideration here—the German, French, and Italian—accomplished its popular breakthrough in sequential decades, and each with a different strategy.[2] The Communist Party of Germany (KPD) emerged in the 1920s as the first mass-based communist party outside of the Soviet Union. It pursued a policy of revolutionary militancy modeled on the Marxism-Leninism of the "classical years" 1917-1921. The KPD eschewed alliances with the reformist Social Democratic Party (SPD) and trade unions and envisioned revolution as a military assault launched by the proletariat against the entrenched fortresses of bourgeois power. The French Communist Party (PCF) achieved mass status in the 1930s on the basis of the popular front policy, which led the communist parties into alliances with socialists and liberals around a program of social reform and the defense of democratic institutions against fascism. Nevertheless, the PCF could never quite fully embrace the implications of its own successful strategy, and in subsequent years it would oscillate between the poles of a popular front-type program, as in the Resistance, and a more intransigent policy that sharply demarcated the PCF from other groups on the left. The Italian Communist Party

(PCI) fought its way to popular status in the anti-fascist resistance. Its activities in these years were based on the national front strategy, which involved the PCI in cross-class alliances even more extensive than those undertaken by the PCF in the 1930s. Under the leadership of Palmiro Togliatti, the PCI by the end of World War II had virtually abandoned the Leninist model of party organization and had come to articulate a gradualist transition from capitalism to socialism.

In the dated but still prevailing interpretive approach to European communism, individual party histories and, more particularly, the evolution of their political strategies, are seen as simply derivative of the Comintern's or, more crassly, Stalin's personal, domination over the international communist movement. Sometimes, this approach is complemented by analyses that give primacy to the major external events during the lifespan of the Comintern—the disruptions unleashed by World War I, the Great Depression and the rise of fascism, the onset of World War II—and their interpretation by the Soviet leadership. In either case, it then becomes a simple matter of ascribing changes in party and Comintern strategies to the personal or collective whims of the Soviet leadership; to changes in Soviet domestic policies, which were immediately carried over to the International; or to Soviet strategic interests. This view originated in the political debates of the 1920s, and then became especially pronounced in post-World War II scholarship.[3]

This mode of explanation is by no means entirely wrong. Obviously, the history of communism cannot be divorced from Soviet developments and, especially, from the rise of Stalinism. The emergence of mass-based communist parties is hardly imaginable outside the crucible of the political and economic crises that virtually defined the first half of the twentieth century. Nonetheless, an interpretive schema focused exclusively on the *Soviet Union*, the *political* orientation of communist parties, and major political *events* is overly simplistic and leaves many more questions unasked and unresolved. Most often, this schema entails a highly deterministic reading of communist history, a political narrative whose beginning and end points are already known. Especially in the older, Cold War-influenced version, political events, *external* to the histories of the parties themselves, serve as the driving factors that summon up predictable responses from the Comintern and the communist parties, as if no other options were open to communist parties and a certain political logic had to prevail for all parties in all instances. Parties are seen as reacting to political events in a reflexive, unmediated manner. The result is a picture of uniformity that masks the varieties of communism (which existed even at the height of Stalinism), ignores the important fact that individual parties had highly varied experiences with the different strategies, and subsumes social into political history. The social context, to the extent that it is present at all, is treated as mere backdrop, its impact on party formation more assumed than explicated, or described in such general terms as to be of limited usefulness.

More recent studies, less encumbered by Cold War politics and aided by wider access to archival sources, have substantially modified this picture by demonstrating the influence of various individuals and parties within the Comintern hierarchy and the intense if intermittent debate that often accompanied strategic shifts.[4] They have more firmly placed the individual parties within their particular national context. But for the most part, they have been no less one-sided than the Cold War histories in their emphasis on political events and on the overtly political dimension of European communism.

This kind of circumscribed political history, without question important in delineating certain aspects of communist history, cannot, however, address why, on the basis of particular strategies, some communist parties were able to make the transition from sect to popular movement. This void has only been partly addressed by the emergence, in the last generation, of social histories of labor that sometimes intersect with communist party history.[5] These social histories, generally centered upon localities or regions, less frequently upon specific industries or even factories, have demonstrated the always imperfect fit between party and class. They have explicated the reasons why communist parties in different situations have been able to garner substantial popular support. But by and large, they have left unexamined the opposite flow: the way that a particular kind of popular base and social setting also shaped the character and strategy of individual communist parties. By focusing so intently on localities and regions, they have redressed the Moscow-centeredness of older party and Comintern histories, but have often failed to link the local with the national and have sometimes ignored altogether the international dimension of European communism. This last is a particularly striking omission in studies of a movement that consciously promoted an international identification among its members, often depended on directives from the Comintern, and while ensconced in particular national traditions, also emerged in the context of trans-national European social developments.[6]

The essay that follows examines comparatively the divergent political strategies by which three European communist parties accomplished their popular breakthroughs. The aim here is to explore the interconnections between political strategies and the social and political context in which they were formulated. In seeking to explain why different strategies "worked" in different countries, I intend to read back through the prisms of communist party formation to the particular patterns of economic development, state power, and political representation. I will forego the needlessly pointed division between social and political history, a division surmounted in many areas of historical inquiry but still quite pronounced in the study of European communism. In place of the polarization between local and Moscow-centered studies, I would like to attempt a cross-national comparison that draws on local and national studies and tries to establish the interrelatedness of political strategies and social histories in the formation of mass, popular movements. For this task, an analysis centered around *political space* is particularly helpful.[7] As I use the term here, political space refers to the social and geographical places in which contestations for power unfold. It signifies both a physically and a socially constructed entity, one that most often involves both a built and bounded area, such as a factory or the streets of a neighborhood, and the way that social actors appropriate the resources of that space in political conflict. In this study, political space means mapping comparatively the sites of successful party and popular activism, such as the workplace, the streets, the household, the village, and the battlefield, as well as the "normal" political institutions of parliament and municipal administration. As will become clear below, each of the parties under consideration here operated within a specific combination of spaces, a factor that significantly shaped the party's strategy and its constituencies, that is, the extent to which it recruited support from male workers, female workers, the unemployed, housewives, the middle class, and peasants.

The focus on political space requires, therefore, a more systematic delineation of the relationship between society and party than is found in the traditional histories of communism. In place of the standard concentration on political *events*, it requires also an exploration of the relation between events and large-scale processes, between contingency and structure. Clearly, communist parties were fundamentally shaped by two world wars and a Great Depression. But even these major events occurred within the context of such longterm factors as the rationalization of European industry, the increasing geographic concentration of working-class populations, the expansion of state capacities, and gendered understandings of political activism that idealized the male proletariat as the heroic revolutionary force.

Furthermore, the focus on political space compels attentiveness to the creative actions of parties and mass movements, their *construction of new*, as well as their utilization of existing, political space. In the language of structure and agency, this entails the recognition that communist parties had to operate within structured conditions over which they had little, if any, control, and also had to seek out new avenues of mobilization and activism.[8] In this context, the use of political space illuminates the critical, ever-present, and often tension-bound connection between spheres of production and reproduction in the mobilizing strategies of mass movements and parties.

Finally, the concept of political space allows for an open-ended consideration of the relationship between political ideology and political practice. As will become clear below, in some instances, political ideology determined the sites in which communist parties operated. In other instances, the parties adapted their ideology and practice to national and social realities, and moved into the available political space. Ideology could be reshaped by practice, practice by ideology.

1

From Armed Revolution to Street Battles: The KPD in the Weimar Republic

The KPD, formed at the very end of 1918, imbibed the messianic radicalism inspired by the Bolshevik Revolution: the sense that 1917 had opened up a new era in world history and that the tasks of the member parties of the Comintern consisted of reenactments of the Russian October.[9] The party sought continually, therefore, to elevate all manifestations of mass activism into assaults on the fundamental structures of bourgeois society. Despite all the internal conflicts of the 1920s, the numerous changes of leadership, and the ultimate defining role of the Comintern, the fundamental commitment to mass activism and armed revolution as the means of social transformation and the concomitant rejection of bourgeois institutions and political alliances cut through the factional divisions of the party.[10]

The rhetorical and practical militancy of the KPD was not merely a Soviet export bought in Germany. Ideologically, the KPD's strategy marked a synthesis of certain aspects of Rosa Luxemburg's thought with Marxism-Leninism. Luxemburg's major bequest to the KPD was not her well-known belief in democratic practices, but a militant voluntarism, a commitment to mass activism so pronounced that demonstrations and strikes were, for her, in and of themselves the highest expression of democracy.[11] In Luxemburg's view, the streets served as the constitutive terrain of political democracy and the primary space of political conflict between the forces of revolution and the forces of order.[12] Strikes were significant precisely because they moved beyond factory and workplace-centered issues to pose the fundamental issue of power in society.[13] The normal political arena of legislatures and municipal councils could only supplement the streets, and then as the site of agitation and propaganda rather than effective, practical work. While Luxemburg's theoretical writings revolve around the breakdown of capitalism and the nationalities issue, the *institutional grounding* of a democratic-socialist polity received precious little attention.[14] Much more frequently, she devoted herself to issues of strategy and tactics—with a rhetorical brilliance that, to be sure, enriched the content of her writings—designed to elevate the intensity of political conflict.[15]

Ideologically, then, the KPD joined the militant voluntarism common to Luxemburg and Lenin with Lenin's emphasis on a disciplined party organization and a powerful central state. By the late

6

1920s, the Luxemburgist-Leninist hybrid was increasingly subject to Stalin's particularly authoritarian interpretation of Leninism.

But the KPD's voluntaristic politics did not derive in pristine fashion from its ideological progenitors. Politically, the KPD's strategy converged with the multiple forms of popular protest that erupted amid the material and political crises unleashed by war, hyperinflation, and depression. Mass activism, however, did not go unchallenged. Amid strikes, demonstrations, and armed rebellions, and demands for socialization, a polity based on workers and soldiers and councils, shorter work days, and more extensive social welfare benefits, a highly tenuous but unmistakable consensus of order coalesced in opposition to the radical left and popular activism. Despite deep disagreements on such fundamental issues as republicanism and social welfare policy, the coalition of order, stretching from the SPD on the left to the conservative nationalist DNVP on the right, proved remarkably durable. It was forged first in opposition to the workers and soldiers councils of 1918/19, sealed through the military repression of the councils, and sustained by the desire to counter the growth of a mass-based communist party. Most basically, the coalition of order promoted the reassertion of state and managerial powers, a strategy often mediated through the SPD and the trade unions, the mainstays of the Weimar system. The reestablishment of order in the course of the 1920s narrowed significantly the space within which popular struggles could unfold, leading to the formation, in the KPD's case, of a party comprised overwhelmingly of unemployed men and confined to the constricted political space of neighborhood streets.

The Revolution of 1918/19, however spontaneous its origins and incomplete its effects, established the precedent of armed political struggle in Germany. In four of the first five years of the Republic, the KPD sought to found a socialist system through military means: the (misnamed) Spartacist Uprising of 1919, the Ruhr conflict that followed the Kapp-Putsch in 1920, the so-called March Action of 1921, and the uprising of October 1923. The Luxemburgist-Leninist commitment to mass action and armed revolution provided the rationale for these efforts, as did the Russian model of one revolution quickly unfolding into a second.

None of these attempts succeeded. But they provided the KPD with its own militaristic legacy, one sustained by the sometime violence of the KPD's political rhetoric and by the individual and political martyrdoms ascribed to its military efforts in subsequent propaganda. In the midst of the March Action, the *Ruhr-Echo*, the local party paper in Essen, ran a banner headline, taken from the penultimate phrase of the party program, written by Luxemburg, "Thumbs in the enemy's eyes, the knee on his chest!"[16] Following the event, *Rote Fahne*, the central KPD paper, proudly trumpeted the Comintern's pronouncement, "You have acted correctly!"[17] The workers killed at Leuna and elsewhere in central Germany in this conflict became the martyred heroes of German communism, as were the Hamburg workers killed in the ill-starred 1923 uprising.[18] By glorifying its own military efforts, despite the string of failures, the KPD sought to join its traditions with the Soviet invocation of the October Revolution and the victorious Civil War as *the* heroic moments of Bolshevism and of world socialism.[19]

After the suppression of the 1923 revolt, the KPD never again attempted an armed uprising. The wellsprings of popular activism had been largely depleted by the devastating series of material crises—war, reconstruction, inflation, stabilization—and by the accompanying intense but inconclusive political conflicts. The popular longing for some semblance of normalcy, coupled with the very clear successes of coordinated repression by government and employers, closed off the option of armed revolt. Nonetheless, the KPD's militaristic ethos intensified in the succeeding years, receiving its clearest expression in the attention lavished on the party's paramilitary organization, the Roter Frontkämpferbund (RFB—Red Front Fighters Association), and on the underground military apparatuses.[20] The party press in these years was infused with militaristic images. The KPD's *Arbeiter-Illustrierte-Zeitung*, for example, published photo after photo of uniformed men, banners flying, marching in tightly disciplined military formation. Only the uniforms and banners enable a viewer to distinguish the RFB from the Nazi SA. One sees the same determined men—women are completely absent in both the KPD and Nazi representations—the same emphasis on a muscular masculinity, and even photos of party leader Ernst Thälmann complete with jackboots and brown cap.[21]

No doubt, the KPD's militaristic ethos intensified through the party's interaction with National Socialism. During the Depression the KPD sought to wean away some of the Nazi Party's constituency by elevating male combativeness to new heights of glory. In so doing, the KPD invoked its own legacy, but also demonstrated its partial absorption of aspects of Nazi rhetoric and practice.[22] Both glorified street combat, even as they fought one another for control of neighborhoods.[23] These street battles of the last years of the Republic became for the KPD a kind of pseudo-revolutionary political practice. If the party was unable to engage in actual armed conflict for control of Germany, then the battle for the streets would constitute the terrain on which the Revolution would be fought. Some party members were aware that street battles and armed revolution were not quite the same thing and that the sense of civil disorder they created might ultimately benefit the Nazis, but for a party schooled on the Luxemburgist-Leninist celebration of mass activism, the specter of thousands of workers in the streets was simply too enticing.

The politics of street battles, with its elevation of physical prowess to the essential revolutionary quality, lent to the KPD a decidedly masculine tone, one only accentuated by the party's idealization of male productive labor as the source of the material riches of society. The *Arbeiter-Illustrierte-Zeitung*, for example, published innumerable depictions glorifying male labor—lathe operators, riggers, riveters, underground construction workers.[24] Female workers are depicted as harried and oppressed, almost never in the heroic cast given to their male counterparts. Wedded to the classically Marxian emphasis on the sphere of production as the bedrock of social organization and the locus of political struggle, the KPD denigrated the individual household as a backward province of petit-bourgeois values, which therefore could never serve as a crucial site of political struggle.[25] Yet for the majority of proletarian women, the household remained the essential space of social life in the Weimar Republic. Impervious to this fact, the KPD and the Comintern argued that women's emancipation would develop only in tandem with their participation in the productive sphere.[26]

As a result, the KPD proved singularly incapable of benefitting from the fact that women's activism and the politicization of gender reached new levels of intensity during the Weimar Republic. According to party statistics, in 1929, the high point, women composed only 17 percent of the membership; in the last years of the Weimar Republic, the figure hovered around 15 percent.[27] The KPD's electoral profile was the most masculine of any party in the Weimar Republic.[28] Even when the KPD occasionally moved beyond its own strategic framework and sought to mobilize women in other arenas, it did so in a haphazard fashion that only underscored the primacy placed on male proletarian militancy. The women's column of the *Arbeiter-Illustrierte-Zeitung* offered household and childcare advice to women. In accord with other political tendencies in the Weimar Republic, the KPD promoted a "rationalized" household in which efficient work and modern technology would combine to ease the burden on women.[29] But the inconsistent publication of the column and its burial in the inner pages of the magazine—following the representations of marching men—only underscored the KPD's ambivalent relationship to women and to the household. The primarily household role of women went largely unquestioned. One issue of *Rote Fahne* in 1920 advised men to send their women to party meetings and told them not to worry that the housework would not be completed. The women's improved morale would help them do their household chores more efficiently.[30] Only two articles in a six-year span of the weekly *Arbeiter-Illustrierte-Zeitung* criticized men's regal bearing around the household and the suppression of women within it.[31] The party's support of food riots and efforts to establish control committees over prices, especially pronounced during 1923, were also inconstant. And in the great campaign against the prohibition of abortion, the KPD attracted significant levels of support that extended far beyond its male proletarian base. Ultimately, however, the KPD, fearful of mass activism that lay beyond its control, pulled back from the movement and thereby sacrificed the potential for a more broadly based constituency.[32] The combined emphasis on male labor and male combativeness, forged in the political space of the battlefield and the streets, left precious little space for the invocation of women's social roles as the basis of a political movement or of the future political order.[33] And it resulted in little sustained attention to the specifics of women's subordination.

As a proletarian-based party, the KPD was of course most concerned with organizing workers in the factories and mines. In fact, the broad and intense labor insurgency that began with the first wartime strikes in 1916 and ended with a failed miners' strike in the spring of 1924—a product of both the existential crises of war and inflation and of the relatively long term, rationalization-derived formation of a geographically and socially concentrated working class—had initially provided the KPD with a fruitful terrain of activity. Within the workplace and from the outside, communists helped to sustain labor protests and sought to elevate the conflicts into a generalized revolutionary movement. "Generallstreik! Heraus aus den Betrieben!" ("General strike! Out of the workplace!") was the KPD's almost Pavlovian response to any labor action.[34] The party often supported the widespread indiscipline of the labor force in these years, and only occasionally bothered to distinguish between criminal and political challenges to authority. At the Leuna chemical works, for example, the substantial KPD cell turned a blind eye toward, and possibly encouraged, endemic petty thievery. More substantively, communist shop stewards and the intermittently communist-dominated Works Council played an important role in contesting management's efforts to impose lower piecework rates and to contain wage increases.[35] Such activity won for the KPD the support of a substantial segment of the working class in some particular enterprises and regions in Germany.

Yet after 1924, the workplace became almost *terra incognita* for the KPD, a most ironic situation for a party whose entire existence and meaning rested on the idealized role of the proletariat and whose organizational structure supposedly rested on enterprise cells. The Luxemburgist-Leninist hostility to the trade unions as bureaucratic, reformist institutions continually drew the party toward building independent trade unions, a practice that became official party and Comintern policy in 1929.[36] But aside from a few local successes, the organization of separate unions weakened the party since the KPD-linked affiliates were never able to supplant the more established unions.

More significantly, the high levels of unemployment that resulted from both rationalization and the onset of the Depression in 1929 seriously undermined the communist presence in the workplace.[37] Rationalization had been a crucial component of managerial strategies in Germany even before World War I. Skilled workers found their relative autonomy on the shop floor under attack while all workers were under heightened pressure to increase their productivity. Moreover, the general expansion of the industrial economy, and in particular the growth of large-scale, bureaucratically managed enterprises, led to the increased geographical concentration of working-class communities, a factor that facilitated widespread popular protest.

While the industrial economy continued to grow, the concerted program of rationalization lapsed during the inflationary period that began with the war and lasted until 1923. But as part of the economic stabilization program initiated in 1923/24, German employers revived with a vengeance their commitment to technological and managerial innovations. After five or six years of almost continual challenges from labor, employers seized on the economic and social crisis to reassert their powers. To management, formal political efforts aimed at securing labor representation in or control over the workplace and the widespread lack of work discipline on the shop floor were pieces of the same radical cloth. They sought to silence labor politically and, at the same time, to reduce their costs of production in an era marked by structural over-capacity in a number of crucial industries and by increased, state-mandated social welfare expenses. Industry's concerted program of rationalization, supported by the state and even by the SPD and trade unions, resulted in longer work days, an intensified pace of work, and substantial layoffs. Indeed, unemployment levels became so high that a segment of the structurally unemployed was created even before 1929, a trend drastically magnified by the demographic bulge of the 1920s and the world economic crisis.[38] Companies used these layoffs to rid their factories and mines of militant workers, communists chiefly, and extended their political control over those who remained employed. At Leuna, for example, where the KPD had had a strong presence in the early 1920s, the company fired communist workers and had police and company security agents patrol the railroad stations used by workers to ensure that KPD leaflets and newspapers were not distributed. When the KPD cell newspaper, *Der Leuna-Prolet*, appeared clandestinely, company managers quickly communicated the fact to government officials, and both worked hard to identify the source of printing and distribution.[39] Similar incidents were played out at companies all over Germany.

As a result, the KPD in the mid-1920s became a party composed disproportionately of the unemployed. Some party officials, well aware of the trend, complained that the Catholic Center and the SPD had become the parties of employed workers, the KPD of the unemployed.[40] By 1932, only 11 percent of the membership was employed.[41] Enterprise cells, the basic organizational structure of the party, were few and far between, and those that did exist were often more fictional than real.[42]

Most seriously, unemployment deprived the affected workers of representation through the workplace-based institutions of the labor movement: the trade unions and works councils.[43] Except for their advocacy of general macroeconomic proposals, neither sought to integrate the demands of the unemployed into their negotiations with employers and the state. Indeed, workplace representation after 1924 became largely the province of Social Democrats and Catholics and an integral part of the corporatist-style arrangements of the Weimar system. Unions won access to the state, notably through state-mandated arbitration of labor disputes, cooperation in the drafting of social legislation, and the management of certain social welfare programs. The fact that the Ministry of Labor and other relevant state offices were often held by Social Democrats or Catholic reformers with trade union roots only facilitated the incorporation of workplace representation into the Weimar system. In sharp contrast, for those who were displaced from the productive sphere or first came of working age in the 1920s and 1930s and were unable to find a foothold in the labor market, the streets served as the only available space through which their grievances could be articulated. The focal point of their actions became government unemployment offices, welfare agencies, and even, in some notorious instances, employed workers—all identified, in part justifiably, with the Social Democratic Party. The KPD, schooled in the Luxemburgist-Leninist emphasis on mass activism and Luxemburg's celebration of the streets, proved more than ready to support the demonstrations of the unemployed, especially as these were so often infused with hostility toward the SPD and the unions.

During the Weimar Republic, the KPD won substantial representation in the Reichstag, state parliaments, and municipal councils. Representative institutions, especially at the communal level, had been crucial sites for the gestation of political opposition in Germany from the early nineteenth century onwards. Yet for most of its history, the KPD, true to its Luxemburgist-Leninist heritage, considered republican institutions mainly as forums for agitation, and the Leninist emphasis on central state power led it to neglect seriously the communal level.

At its founding convention and over the objections of Luxemburg and others, the KPD decided not to contest the upcoming election for the Constitutional Assembly, arguing that such involvement indicated an acceptance of bourgeois institutions. This revolutionary purism did not last beyond the first national election of the Weimar Republic, but the party's dim estimation of parliamentary work did not change substantially. Ruth Fischer's opening salutation to the Reichstag in 1924, "Hochverehrtes Affentheater!" (Highly honored ape theater!)—greeted with cackles of delight by the KPD delegation—was perhaps an extreme case and symptomatic of the KPD in its ultra-leftist phase, but it was not untypical.[44]   In Essen in 1924, Communist city councillors refused to take the oath of allegiance to the Weimar Constitution, offering the Prussian Minister of the Interior an easy means of excluding communist officials.[45] Never in the course of the Weimar Republic did the KPD develop a complete program for municipal work.[46]

In some instances, communists did seek to make better use of republican institutions, as in the state governments of Saxony and Thüringia in 1922 and 1923 and intermittently between 1925 and 1928 throughout the Reich. But even at these moments the KPD viewed democratic politics more in an instrumental fashion, as a means of accelerating the onset of the ultimate revolutionary conflict.[47] The quick slide from practical work to utter rejection of representative bodies with the onset of the more radical tactics of the "third period" in 1928 is indicative of how tentatively the KPD viewed is activities in the parliamentary sphere. No party faction in the 1920s ever recognized any kind of substantive value in democratic institutions, and party work within them was always secondary to the more enticing prospects of combat in the streets. Moreover, in the rare instances when KPD representatives were chosen for municipal administrative posts (not just as councillors), the state ministries of the interior most often refused to confirm the appointments.[48]

The denigration of practical involvement in the political institutions of the nation closed off the one site through which a modus vivendi with other social groups could have been reached. Problems of housing and mass transportation, of water supplies and electricity rates, were community issues whose impact extended far beyond the proletariat. Yet with very few exceptions, the party had virtually no base in the countryside or among the middle class. According to party statistics, industrial workers composed about 80 percent of the party membership in 1928.[49] Rhetorical paeans to the potential revolutionary character of the peasantry and the impoverished petit-bourgeoisie had little meaning, especially when the ideology, program, and strategy of the KPD revolved so clearly around the proletariat.

For all the limited political space in which it operated, the KPD nonetheless became the first mass-based communist party outside of the Soviet Union. The primacy it placed on action accorded with the sensibilities of a significant segment of the male working-class population driven to the margins of economic and social life by rationalization, state welfare policies, and economic crisis. Since the unemployed so often attributed their plight to the SPD, the party most closely identified with the Weimar system, the KPD, with its own, ideologically-based hostility to social democracy, became the logical vehicle for their discontent.[50] The KPD's commitment to the streets as the essential space of political conflict—once it had been driven from the battlefield and the workplace, and had chosen to ignore the household and to reject republican institutions—and its promotion of male combativeness converged with the fact that the unemployed had no space other than the streets through which they could articulate their grievances and demands. At the same time, the KPD's support for a powerful central state, the dictatorship of the proletariat in its specifically Marxist-Leninist guise, seemed to offer the unemployed the means of surmounting their dire social situation and accorded with a long tradition of German political practice that granted the state a powerful role in the construction of society. Yet the party's strategy and ideology ultimately restricted it to a constituency composed largely of the male unemployed. From this group, intense if sporadic political conflict could be expected, but an effective politics became an ever more distant prospect.

2

Intransigence and Integration: The PCF and the Popular Front

The 1930s began inauspiciously for the French Communist Party.[51] The French government had launched a highly effective campaign of repression against the party, with the result that virtually the entire leadership sat in prison. Lacking the strong intellectual underpinnings provided by a Rosa Luxemburg or an Antonio Gramsci, the PCF proved particularly susceptible to personnel rearrangements and strategic shifts emanating from Moscow. Rarely, if ever, did the party work through the intellectual rationale or longterm consequences of such shifts, giving to French communism a hue of political opportunism from which it has never been free.

In 1927, the Comintern had imposed on the PCF an ultra-leftist strategy—the "third period" strategy or, as it was known in France, "class against class"—that was particularly ill-suited to the task of building a mass party in a country with deeply-rooted republican traditions and a highly diverse social structure in which the proletariat would never constitute anything close to a majority of the population.[52] Nonetheless, "class against class" marked an important period in the development of French communism. As membership rolls and electoral support dwindled, the PCF became a more disciplined organization. Party militants gained crucial organizational experience in the adverse circumstances of government and employer repression in the 1920s and early 1930s. Even with a strategy so ill-conceived as class against class, they built some solid bases of support in a few enterprises and municipalities, especially in the Paris suburbs and the northern industrial regions, and in some rural areas with a strong left-wing tradition.[53]

The French Communist Party was, then, well poised to take advantage of another Comintern shift, that to the Popular Front.[54] In the Popular Front the PCF entered into an alliance first with the Socialist Party (Section Française de l'Internationale Ouvrière-SFIO) and then with the Radical Party as well. The goals were quite modest: social and political reforms that spoke to the interests of the *classes moyennes* as well as the proletariat, and which were fully consonant with the functioning of a bourgeois democratic system. Hardly a revolutionary movement in its origins, the Popular Front sought to invigorate republican institutions in a period in which they were under siege from the effects of economic crisis and the rise of fascist movements at home and abroad. But the electoral victory of the popular front parties in the spring of 1936 unleashed a popular upsurge that pushed the Popular Front far beyond its initial, rather modest goals.[55] The tangible, material benefits that workers derived from these measures were short-lived. The long term changes inscribed into France's political landscape were highly significant. As a political party coalition and a mass movement, the Popular Front opened up to the PCF the political spaces of the Third Republic. But by accommodating itself to the institutions of the Republic, the PCF inscribed into its own history an unresolvable tension between intransigent Leninism and republican integration.

Unlike the KPD, the PCF, even in its most radical phases, could never quite completely denigrate the importance of the electoral sphere and representative institutions, a sure sign of the intractable importance of French republicanism. Despite the continual stream of criticism from the Comintern, which often charged the PCF with "electoralism," French communists engaged in elections and administrative work with a seriousness that far surpassed their more militant comrades across the Rhine.[56] Already in the 1920s the PCF had been able to win control of municipal administration in a number of communes. In the 1935 local elections, the first electoral test of the Popular Front, the party vastly increased its penetration of the local political arena, doubling the number of municipalities it controlled from 150 to 297. In the Paris suburbs alone the PCF won control of 27 out of 79 municipalities.[57] There the PCF established itself in new or expanded residential areas that were characterized by the geographical concentration of industrial workers and extremely poor living conditions. Communities like Bobigny lacked even the basic infrastructures of sewer lines, utilities, paved streets, and schools. Local communists, working through neighborhood associations and the electoral process, succeeded in providing basic services to the residents, along with unemployment assistance, vacation colonies, and public health centers.[58] The PCF thereby acquired a sense of identity with the local residents and a solid political base. As Tyler Stovall writes:

> Community activism was to a significant extent Communist activism in Bobigny, and it was this kind of activism that gave the town's working class allotment areas much of their sense of identity. The PCF thus both helped develop community sentiment in Bobigny and benefitted from it politically.[59]

By using the tools of the electoral process and local administration, the PCF became ensconced within one of the hallowed spaces of French republicanism, the commune. Through the articulation of community issues, the PCF was able to attract support beyond the male proletariat, at least in the localities that it controlled politically. In contrast, a politics focused on the battlefield and the streets, as was the case with the KPD, could never speak to the concerns of the lower middle class or women. White-collar employees in the Paris suburbs, faced with housing conditions little different from that of industrial workers, were in some instances willing to support the PCF because of its success in improving municipal services, a process facilitated by the nationalistic and republican tone of communist politics during the Popular Front.[60] In Bobigny, despite initial hostility between local merchants and the communists, the municipality constructed marketplaces for the local merchants, and during the Popular Front joined with the well-organized local branch of the PCF front, the Confédération du Petit Commerce et de l'Artisanat, in launching a campaign in defense of small merchants and in calling for unemployment benefits to be paid to small merchants and artisans. In the midst of the employment crisis of the Depression, communists were able to organize with other groups in the city, including the Church and lower middle class elements, to provide support for the unemployed. In turn, the merchants and artisans became integrated into the social and cultural life of the commune that was so much a feature of the communist-controlled municipalities.[61]

Control of the local state, along with participation in the Chamber of Deputies, also constituted the space within which the PCF articulated a reconstructed understanding of gender, a vital aspect of its integration into national institutions. Until the Popular Front, the political rhetoric of the PCF, no less than the KPD, centered on the heroic male proletariat, and the household sphere, analytically and politically, barely figured into communist activity. In its efforts to expand its influence among women, the party, convinced despite the evidence that French industry was becoming increasingly dependent on female labor, concentrated on women workers.[62] And in sharp contrast to virtually all other political groups in France, the PCF prior to 1934 espoused a neo-Malthusian approach to the population issue. That is, it viewed family limitation as an acceptable strategy that would enable working-class families to improve their material situation and would provide them with more time to engage in the class struggle.

Yet in a significant departure from communist practice, the PCF in the Popular Front abandoned this approach, so out of step with the dominant French discourse on gender and the family. Instead, it adopted a highly conventional view of sexuality and a pronatalist position that gave primacy to women's maternal and household roles.[63] The PCF now linked its critique of capitalism with France's supposed demographic crisis: It indicted capitalist society for creating the conditions that made it difficult for the French to support large families, thereby endangering the very future of the nation.

The PCF's new position became evident in *L'Humanité* in the winter of 1935-36. In a series of articles on the issue of the family, the paper's editor, Paul Vaillant-Couturier, defined the party's task as "mak[ing] motherhood a social function of the highest order. . . because upon it depends the continuity and improvement of the species."[64] Similarly, during the 1936 strikes, the PCF leader Jacques Duclos, in language evocative of the more generalized pronatalist discourse, called on "the women of France to unite for the protection of their homes" and for "the future of the race."[65] And party leader Maurice Thorez himself gave expression to the new PCF position at a national conference in 1937:

> Finally, we are worried about the crisis of depopulation that saps our people. Our hopes reside in the children. . . and we *want* our workers, our peasants, to *be able* to have many children, we want fathers and mothers to be able to raise their dear families [*leur petite famille*] suitably. Our party, our municipalities, have done a great deal in this regard, but it is necessary to establish a national policy for the protection of children, of maternity, of the family, as our conference has demanded. On that depends the future of the race.[66]

Moreover, while the PCF in the pre-Popular Front period had dismissed the public display of sexually suggestive art and advertisements as a sign of bourgeois degeneration, now its own popular weekly, *Regards*, devoted more and more space to such "feminine" topics as beauty, household economics, and creams and ointments. Its standards became elevated as well. While the KPD's popular weekly in the 1920s depicted oppressed women and utilitarian proletarian fashions, *Regards* displaying haute coiffeure and haute couture in its pages. Even women workers on strike exhibited a kind of elegance, and female nudes were sometimes displayed.[67] Film stars like Claudette Colbert came to grace the pages of this PCF magazine.[68] At the same time, the party weekly linked together health, beauty, and maternalism, which together would promote sound families engaged in the national cause of population development.[69]

In the political sphere primarily, not the workplace, the PCF articulated its new-found support of pronatalism and its conventional notions of sexuality. The workplace offered only limited possibilities for organizing women, as the PCF in the 1930s implicitly recognized. The proportion of female participation in the paid industrial labor force declined throughout the interwar years in France[70]—a consequence of the growing importance of heavy industries like mining and metallurgy that prized male labor, a concerted effort to secure jobs for men during the demobilization following World War I as well as during the Depression, and the general pronatalist content of the French discourse on gender and the family, which provided an ideological rationale for returning women to the home to ensure the future survival of the nation. Even the great workplace mobilizations of 1936 (to be discussed below) had a particularly ephemeral impact on the longterm party and union organization of women.[71]

But the PCF's occupation of political space in the legislature and, especially, the municipalities, provided it with a powerful platform from which it could articulate and implement policies that addressed the multiple interests of women—as homemakers, mothers, spouses, and workers. Public health facilities, summer camps for children, community parks, even daycare centers—all were supported in the pronatalist terms of French political discourse. These facilities, by providing for the health and safety of women and children, would ensure the procreation and survival of the nation.

Similarly, the acquisition of many more parliamentary seats in the 1936 election enabled the PCF to propose legislation that won a wide hearing. Its 1936 bill for "'effective protection of maternity and childhood'" proposed measures that "hardly anyone could oppose," including the creation of a national office for coordinating programs that supported women and children and new legislation that "'would protect mothers effectively before, during and after pregnancy,' encourage breastfeeding, and protect all children through three years of age."[72] In later proposals, the PCF also called for the panoply of measures designed to promote large families that had become a fixture of pronatalist demands in France, such as state-provided bonuses that increased with more children, subsidies, and tax breaks. Significantly, the party abandoned in this bill its earlier support of legalized abortion and of easier access to contraception. Pointedly, Thorez stated that he did not want the PCF to repeat the error of the KPD, which through its advocacy of abortion rights had handed the Nazis a valuable political weapon against the party.[73]

Thus, in the words of François Delpla, the PCF managed the "very laborious constitution of a pronatalist common front."[74] In so doing, the PCF, unlike the KPD, recognized the crucial political significance of the household, but as a space to be protected rather than as a site of political mobilization. Nonetheless, the evolution of the party's views on gender and the family were just as critical as its recognition of republican realities in inserting the PCF into French society, an evolution mediated through the occupation of political space in the municipalities and the Chamber of Deputies.[75]

While the PCF's conquest of political space provided it with an arena in which it could articulate and implement its ideas on gender, the conquest of a base in the economic sphere was crucial to its ability to garner support among industrial workers, males in particular. Here also, the communist success in the Popular Front era built upon earlier gains, and upon the specific character of French economic development in the interwar years.

During the 1920s France largely escaped the stagnation that burdened other industrial economies in this period. Instead, it experienced an inflation-fueled advance of the industrial sector that transformed the structure of the French economy.[76] Some of France's traditional industries survived well, but the overall balance shifted more toward the modern sector as French industry became more diversified, more capital intensive, and more highly rationalized. Even the Depression did not significantly interrupt the transformation of the French economy. Significantly, unemployment, in comparative terms, remained fairly low.[77] Technological rationalization and the Depression did not, then, remove from the workplace on an almost permanent basis a substantial segment of the French labor force. The French working class remained highly heterogeneous, but the fault line did not run between the employed and the unemployed, as in Germany in the 1920s and 1930s, and the PCF never became a party of the unemployed.

Yet conditions were hardly rosy for French workers in the interwar period. France's comparatively low jobless rate provided small comfort to the large number of workers who did experience unemployment. Real wages declined significantly during the Depression. And the technological and managerial innovations adopted in the 1920s and 1930s resulted, if not in structural unemployment, then certainly in a more intense pace of work, greater managerial supervision, and, in general, the exercise of overwhelming and arbitrary powers on the part of the *patronat*. As in Germany, rationalization served the twin ends of lowering the costs of production and securing and extending managerial powers in the workplace. In the auto industry, this entailed attacks on the relative autonomy of skilled workers through closer supervision, the expansion of assembly line production, higher production rates, and, during the Depression, pay reductions.[78] In the mines, rationalization signified the adoption of the longwall method in place of the traditional room and pillar system. With the longwall system, large numbers of workers used machinery along a single coal face.[79] This permitted much closer supervision of the miners, and the adoption of the Taylor-derived Bedaux system, which enabled managers to break down the tasks of mining and to pay workers at individual rates of production. *Chronometrages*, tightly controlled timekeeping of specific tasks, was a crucial element of the Bedaux method, and affected both miners and factory workers. While company engineers and management touted the new work methods, factory workers and miners came to view the workplace as alien space in which they were deprived of all rights and all legitimate representation.[80]

By 1936, an accumulation of workplace grievances and the fear of unemployment enveloped the consciousness of French workers. At the same time, the structural transformations of the economy in the interwar period had created more geographically concentrated working-class communities, some levelling of skill distinctions, and, in many places, close links between the workplace and community—conditions that, as in Germany in an earlier period, enhanced the capacity of workers to engage in mass activism. The unification in early 1936 of the two trade union federations, the socialist CGT and the communist CGTU, and then the Popular Front electoral victory resulted in a renewed burst of confidence on the part of workers. The new confidence plus pent-up grievances proved an explosive combination that led to the great strikes of May and June 1936. Though these were largely spontaneous in their origins, experienced communist militants often provided leadership and organizing skills.[81] Through the famed Matignon Agreement and subsequent legislation, workers achieved the right of collective bargaining, wage increases, paid vacations, and the forty-hour week. In many industries, specific agreements extended the reach of workers' gains. In the mines, for example, workers won limits on timekeeping and common pay for longwall mining, though the Bedaux system itself was not banned.[82] Continual labor unrest in the succeeding months served to extend further the wage gains, while the CGT, responding to pressure from below, prevailed upon Blum to implement the forty-hour law in a far more blanket fashion than he had originally envisioned.[83]

While the KPD had been largely removed from the productive sphere, the great labor upsurge of 1936 in France provided the PCF with a much wider entrée into the workplace than previously. In 1934 the party had 450 factory cells, in 1937 around four thousand.[84] These enterprise cells were crucial in developing and maintaining the working-class character of the PCF.[85] Within the factories, the cells were strengthened by the vast increase in union membership, which had been prompted by the unification of the CGT and CGTU in March

1936 and the strike wave the following May and June. Even though some of this membership gain proved temporary, the CGT could still hold on to a power base in the factories, as the election of workers' delegates in the factories indicates.[86]   Moreover, communist-controlled municipalities provided critical strike support, actions that expressively linked workplace and community organization.[87] Politicization went hand in hand with unionization, and the conquest of political space in localities and in the economic sector proved mutually reinforcing.

The achievements of the Popular Front were, to be sure, ephemeral. Wage increases won by workers in the Matignon Agreement were eroded by inflation; little dent was made in unemployment. A general counteroffensive against the labor advances of 1936 soon united employers and government. Combative labor strikes marked 1937 and 1938 no less than 1936. But the joyous atmosphere that pervaded the earlier strikes was little in evidence afterwards. Strikes became more bitter, the mood more sullen, as employers used the panoply of weapons at their command—arbitrary firings, wage reductions, lockouts—to cow their ill-disciplined labor forces. In the mines, the inroads workers had made in 1936 against rationalization measures were reversed, especially under the Daladier government, as employers regained the upper hand and reinstituted the measures they had earlier conceded.[88]   Even the system of state-sponsored arbitration soon turned against workers as employers, following the fall of the Blum government in 1937, added to their own arsenal the weapons of state power. Arbitration decisions unfavorable to workers served as the most benign examples of employer-influenced state policies. More ominous was the deployment by the Daladier government of armed police and soldiers against strikers in 1938.[89] When "l'ordre règne dans l'industrie française,"[90] it was definitely not the kind envisioned by workers in 1936.

But if the specific gains were not long lasting, aside from the famous example of paid vacations, the Popular Front should not therefore be seen as having only symbolic and mythical significance for the French left.[91]   The victory of the Popular Front accelerated a process of politicization that reconfigured the French political landscape, most notably in the emergence of the PCF as a national party occupying vital sites of political space. Yet this was political space made available by the institutions and values of Third Republic France. The alliance of the left reverberated with the symbols of a republicanism founded on revolution; the use of the electoral sphere and the tools of the local and central state constituted on the part of the PCF a recognition of the intractable reality of republican institutions.

The adoption of a pronatalist position inscribed the PCF into the reigning discourse on gender. Only in the workplace did the party carve out new institutional space with the establishment of enterprise cells and the vast expansion of union organization.

By conquering political space that it had not itself mapped, the PCF became enmeshed by its own successes. Enterprise cells, for example, were party institutions. But unions were bipolar institutions: integrated into the party, they were also integrated into the state structure through compulsory collective bargaining and mechanisms for state arbitration. Activities in such corporatist institutions as the Conseil National Économique, charged with a wide range of powers over labor relations by the 1936 legislation, or in the nationalized aircraft industry, inevitably served to moderate the Leninist inclinations of party militants.[92] In the municipalities, the reformist activities of the PCF hardly conjured up the vision of party militants storming the Elysée, the French equivalent of the Winter Palace. Instead of challenging the existing structures of power, the PCF became enmeshed within them as the scope of state power expanded in the popular front—the state became the guarantor of expanded social rights and the social function of women as mothers, and took on a more active economic role through the institutionalization of collective bargaining. The French political structure, centralized as it has been, nonetheless proved quite elastic and porous so long as the PCF shed its overtly revolutionary hide.[93]

But the PCF was also, of course, a member of the Communist International. Marxism-Leninism provided its ideological anchor, Leninism-Stalinism its organizational ballast. Its members were schooled on the stalinized texts of the 1930s and 1940s and trained to accept the Stalinist version of democratic centralism with its premium on discipline, loyalty to the Soviet Union, and an ideological disposition toward the heroic revolutionary strains of Marxism as revised by the Bolshevik Party and by Stalin. At the same time, the party's success through the Popular Front created a different tradition—of leftist unity and radical republicanism—that could only imperfectly be assimilated into the Marxist-Leninist-Stalinist-inspired characteristics of the PCF.[94]

Hence, the ambiguous, even contradictory policies that have marked the history of the PCF derive not only from its diverse intellectual and programmatic legacy—Marxism-Leninism-Stalinism as well as twentieth-century radical republicanism, or, to put it in strategic terms, third period policies versus popular front policies, the revolutionary temper of Marxism-Leninism versus the moderate reformism of the Popular Front. The functional role of the PCF as acquired in the Popular Front has underpinned its strategic oscillation ever since.[95] While the party members have been schooled in the intransigent revolutionary ideology of the Bolshevik Revolution, the party's integration into the institutions of state and society has placed a premium on practical reforms, on the goods the PCF could deliver to its supporters through its occupation of political space in the unions, the municipalities, and the Chamber of Deputies. These the PCF have been loathe to forego for the chimera of proletarian revolution.

3

The Politicization of Civil Society: The PCI in the Resistance and Reconstruction

At the outbreak of World War II, the PCI had been reduced to a party of about three thousand members. The leadership and much of the rank and file languished in exile or in Mussolini's prisons. The party's presence in Italy was almost nonexistent. Yet small groups of activists had managed to remain at large in the country, and from this small nucleus the PCI would emerge in 1945 as a party with nearly two million members and a presence in almost all the important sectors of Italian society.

The PCI's powerful position at the end of World War II derived, of course, from its leading role in the anti-fascist Resistance. The Comintern's national front strategy, which set the party's direction in the Resistance, drew the PCI into alliances with socialists, Catholics, liberals, and even conservative monarchists. Like other communist parties at the time, the PCI moderated its program, symbolized most expressively by the *svolta di Salerno* (the switch of Salerno) by which the party in 1944 entered into the governing coalition presided over by conservatives. The PCI's revolutionary tendencies became even more muted in the postwar years as it sought to maintain the political coalition of the Resistance years and espoused a program that envisaged a gradualist transition from capitalism to socialism.

But the Resistance was far more than a party-led political and military conflict. The Resistance was also a broad-based popular insurgency that, by its very nature, entailed the politicization of virtually all arenas of civil society. In Italy especially, the workplace, the household, and the countryside, alongside the battlefield, constituted the crucial sites of political struggle against the home-grown fascist dictatorship and its unloved German ally. By its promotion of multiple forms of popular mobilization, the PCI conquered extensive areas of political space and attracted a relatively broad and varied constituency. In this manner, the PCI's political practice drew upon the ideological and strategic orientation that Antonio Gramsci and Palmiro Togliatti had begun to define in the mid-1920s and that Gramsci developed further in his prison writings. In turn, the broad-based character of popular mobilization in the

Resistance and in the years of reconstruction (1945-47) served to sustain the Gramscian emphasis on the construction of hegemony in civil society and on revolution as a social process rather than a singular military assault. Ironically enough, the vitality of Italian civil society was also in part the creation of the fascist regime.

As nowhere else in Europe, the workplace served as a central site of political struggle in the Italian Resistance.[96] The first important wartime strike broke out in a Piedmontese glassworks in June 1942.[97] In the following months the incidence of strikes intensified, culminating in a large scale general strike that broke out in March 1943 in the northern cities.[98] Strikes virtually defined the crucial forty-five-day period, in the summer and autumn of 1943, between the fall of Mussolini and the German occupation, erupted again in November and December of 1943, and became still more frequent in 1944 and 1945. The strike of March 1944 paralyzed virtually all of northern Italy, and was the most extensive mass movement in German-occupied Europe. In addition, workers sabotaged the production of war material and defended their factories against Nazi efforts to transport machinery and goods to Germany—the latter a revival, in drastically altered circumstances, of the productivist ideology of the 1920 factory occupations.

While workplace struggles erupted at first over material grievances, they quickly assumed a political character—not surprisingly, since the increasingly dire conditions of life were clearly and inextricably bound up with the policies of the fascist regime. By 1943, whatever enthusiasm Italians had shared at the prospects of a Mediterranean empire had long since faded. Instead, hyperinflation, shortages of essential goods, unemployment, and the pressing reality of war—men who did not return home, deportations to the north, troops criss-crossing the land, aerial bombardments—defined daily life.

In the wrenching context of total war, the PCI provided leadership and political direction. Even in the initial strikes, which were spontaneous in their origins, individual communists within the factories quickly assumed important organizing roles and helped workers reestablish their traditional representative forms, the factory internal commissions.[99] Overwhelmingly, these bodies became dominated by the PCI. The actions of communists within the factories were encouraged by the reestablishment within Italy of the party organization and by the decision, made in September 1943 by the PCI and other groups, to launch armed resistance.[100] Within just a few months, Resistance leaders had begun to connect the burgeoning partisan war with working-class opposition in the factories, a trend signified by the decision to establish clandestine bodies of the

Committee of National Liberation (CLN) within the factories. Communists formed the leadership of the vast majority of these committees of agitation, which only reinforced the PCI's domination of the internal commissions. As the Nazis initiated massive and systematic deportations to Germany in response to workplace militancy, many Italian men fled the cities and joined the partisan armies.[101] The "road to the mountains" often led directly from the factories. By the beginning of 1945, as one historian has written: "The boundaries between the guerrillas in the mountains and the daily actions of the workers who had remained in the factories had become indistinct."[102]

But the crucial role of the workplace in the establishment of the PCI as a mass party depended not only on the contingent events of World War II. Massive working-class opposition and the leading role of the party in the Resistance derived also from the general social and economic policies of the fascist regime. Mussolini's dictatorship promoted the very substantial growth of the industrial economy, including the crucial industries of the "second industrial revolution." As in France, the restructuring of the economy was not seriously interrupted by the Depression, since the impact of the economic crisis was to begin with not as great as in other countries, and the state's active promotion of war-related industries and rescue and absorption of the major banks served to limit further its effects.[103]

While Germans in the 1920s and early 1930s were displaced from the workplace, the sheer growth of the industrial economy expanded the size of the Italian proletariat, a trend that accelerated with the onset of World War II. The war-primed economic boom drew ever greater numbers of Italians, including a large proportion of women, into the ring of the industrial economy. But growth was also accompanied by rationalization measures that aroused intense grievances on the part of workers.[104] As in Germany and France, rationalization entailed closer managerial supervision of the work process, wider implementation of the assembly line, and a generally intensified pace of work. In the familiar pattern, the labor force became somewhat more homogeneous with the emergence of the semi-skilled mass production worker, male or female, as the "classic" proletarian.

Industrial expansion and rationalization signified also the creation of still more concentrated working-class communities, especially since the regime did virtually nothing to lessen the divide between north and south in Italy. In the famed industrial triangle, workplace grievances based on longterm economic transformations combined with the intensely experienced wartime deterioration in living circumstances. Strikes and demonstrations, sit-ins and food riots developed in tandem. The PCI's decision toward the end of 1942 to build street as well as factory cells marked the party's recognition of the linkage between community and workplace and the effort to forge still closer organizational ties between them.[105] The syndicalist ideology and program of Italian fascism served to underscore further the centrality of the workplace. Many state social welfare programs were channeled through the firms, which mediated between workers and the state.[106] Forms of labor representation, however shallow, also survived within the factories, and were strengthened just prior to the outbreak of the war. Individual disputes were most often handled at the enterprise level despite the elaborate arbitration mechanism established by the 1926 law.[107] Following his reinstitution in power by the Germans and the formation of the Republic of Salò, Mussolini sought to reconstitute the popular basis of his regime by recognizing the internal commissions. At the beginning of 1944, he also proposed a socialization measure that envisaged significant workplace representation.[108] Although these measures were rejected by workers, who boycotted workplace elections called by the fascist regime,[109] the rhetoric of labor representation and the general idealization of labor, as in the Fascist Charter, served to underscore the centrality of the workplace. Italian workers turned this phenomenon against the regime by using the workplace as a site of opposition, a strategy that converged with the primacy the PCI placed upon the proletariat as the leading force in the creation of a new society and the sphere of production as the bedrock of social organization.

But the workplace and community were not the only arenas of political conflict that supplemented the battlefield and partisan war as the focal points of the Resistance. The household as political space and women as political actors also became crucial components of the Italian Resistance and the PCI's emergence as a mass party.

The PCI had articulated from its very inception women's issues as part of its strategy. In a manner typical of the communist parties, it initially focused its attention on working women, and at the same time accepted a rather conventional notion of separate spheres that reproduced ideas of women's innate capacity to "create and render pleasant and restful intimacy, the home, the family."[110] In argument with bourgeois feminists, Ruggiero Grieco, who headed the party's women's section, denied the possibilities of women's oppression within the household:

> Our women. . . are burdened with all the evils that place the
> proletariat in slavery. The women are not "slaves of men," as the
> feminists say. Only in rare, pathological cases do men give

offense to women through force and power. The woman is the slave of a situation that the "male" proletariat did not create and of which he is also victim.[111]

In the Resistance, however, the PCI moved away from the exclusive focus on working women and began to redefine its understanding of the subordination of women—a shift inspired by the convergence of female political activism and the party's own efforts to promote resistance through all spheres of society.

The supremely difficult conditions of life during the war affected women in all of their social roles. As homemakers they could not procure food and other essentials for their families; as wives and mothers, they endured the departure of male relations sent off to fight in the regime's ill-fated attempts at foreign conquest or impressed to work in factories in Germany. Moreover, the initial wartime boom and the shortage of male labor, as mentioned above, drew many more women into the industrial economy. In the Piedmont in 1942, for example, 26 percent of the paid industrial labor force was composed of women. Then the economic dislocation beginning in 1943 led to serious unemployment that disproportionately affected women. By the last phase of the war, women and youth together counted for half of the unemployed in the region.[112] Hence, as industrial workers, women experienced the harsh conditions of labor in modern, rationalized factories and the difficulties of unemployment.

Moreover, the fascist regime had politicized womanhood. The regime's hysteria about demographic decline had led it to initiate a panoply of measures designed to increase the birthrate.[113] Women were subjected to a barrage of propaganda reminding them of their duty to the nation: to produce more children and to tend the hearth. Mussolini's exhortation, "War is to man what motherhood is to woman," was not intended only to inspire the combativeness of Italian men.[114] At the same time, many women were mobilized into fascist mass organizations, and took advantage of the increased educational opportunities offered by the regime. As Martin Clark remarks: "In the long run the Fascist regime probably helped, rather than hindered, female emancipation."[115]

Hence, women's extensive participation in the Resistance derived from both the intense material crisis of the war years and a relatively longterm politicization that owed a great deal to the ideology and character of Italian Fascism. The fluid and antibureaucratic nature of resistance activity, which left so much to individual initiative or to the actions of small groups, facilitated the participation of women.[116] Some women fought with the armed partisan units, such as PCI's Garibaldi Brigade or the left liberal Giustizia e Libertà; perhaps more significant is the fact that women lent to the Resistance their own forms of activism: their resistance activities had, as one historian has put it, their own "physiognomy."[117] Women demonstrated for peace and bread, as on International Women's Day in 1943, 1944, and especially 1945, and their actions sparked additional protest strikes and demonstrations. They demonstrated and collected petitions against the deportation of male laborers to Germany and against massacres carried out by the Germans. Women provided crucial links between the extraordinary realm of guerilla forces and more "normal" social arenas. They smuggled arms and food to resistance forces; hid men as they moved from the city to the mountains to join the fighters; and provided support for families of partisans and deportees. As workers they participated in strikes, and as housewives and mothers they provided strike support for the many, many industrial conflicts that were themselves a part of the resistance. Their actions were often designed to ensure the survival of their own households and their various members, particularly males threatened with deportation as forced laborers or combatants, or males subject to political persecution.

The nature of resistance activities thereby politicized the household. As both a geographic space and a social entity, the household became as much a part of the public realm of political contestation as the workplace and the battlefield. Hence, the nature of the Resistance further intensified the politicization of women and brought gender issues to the forefront of Italian politics.

The PCI, which supported the widespread activism of women in the Resistance, proved able to win substantial support among them, despite the strong Catholicism and traditionalism of Italian culture.[118] And the resistance of women pushed the PCI into a subtle but significant reevaluation of its position on women's equality. The broad-based character of women's political activity forced the party to abandon its earlier economistic concentration on women as workers. Moreover, the PCI, at least for a while, gave more explicit recognition to inequalities within the family. In a major departure from standard communist practice, the PCI leadership in 1944 decided to allow separate male and female cells at the base of the party structure, an indication of the heightened awareness of the specificity of women's subordination and of the greater politicization of women in the Resistance.[119] In the PCI-dominated Union of Italian Women (UDI), women promoted issues and demands that, according to one scholar, "contained an analysis of the subordination of women that anticipated by thirty years the proposals and debates on the reforms of the family code."[120] *Noi Donne*, the UDI's paper, demanded female suffrage, equal pay for equal work, and the right of women "to occupy leading positions in the factories, in the schools, in offices, in the countryside."[121] While reaffirming the importance of the family as the fundamental base of society, the UDI in 1944 also levelled a clear critique of the existing institution of the family by proposing reforms of the civil code that would abolish the legally sanctioned powers of males within the family and the disparate treatment of adultery.[122] In addition, Togliatti in the 1940s was arguing that the oppression of women resulted from not only economic but also civil relations, which in the family created a situation of inequality and oppression. Hence, the emancipation of women was not an issue only for one class, but for all women and part and parcel of the profound social transformation that the PCI intended to implement.[123]

Finally and more briefly, another arena of activism for the Italian communists, one that had little parallel elsewhere in the Europe during the Resistance, was the countryside. Fascist economic policy had done virtually nothing to undermine the very heterogeneous character of Italian society with its markedly uneven development. Yet the invocation of the glories of rural life ran up against the trenchant realities of grinding peasant poverty and landlord power that the fascist regime helped to sustain. The continued existence of a substantial and often impoverished non-proletarian sector made it patently clear to the PCI that a politics focused solely on the proletariat, as was the case with the KPD, could never win the majority of the working population—a position with which Gramsci in particular, by personal experience and theoretical reflection, had endowed the party.

Hence, the PCI moved quickly to promote peasant mobilization as part of the Resistance. The PCI sought to defend the immediate interests of the rural population, and to articulate its efforts in terms of the popular struggle against the German occupation. In Emilia, for example, peasants and agricultural laborers, with the active inducement of the party, carried out a grain strike against the Nazis by leaving crops in the field or hiding them. By refusing to thresh, *l'Unità* argued, the peasants "defend not only their own legitimate interests, but fight a great national battle and struggle to assure bread for the Italian people."[124] In Modena, communist partisans distributed foodstuffs to the population and prevented the Germans from requisitioning livestock.[125] In other instances, the PCI supported strikes among landless agricultural laborers, an effort to link the urban and rural Resistance.

In the very different conditions of the south, the first rural land occupations occurred in the autumn of 1943, close on the heels of the advance of Allied forces. The cooperatives that were formed almost spontaneously in this context provided the PCI with the political space through which it could further promote and organize the peasant movement.[126] The PCI's participation in the government beginning in 1944 also proved crucial, for its Minister of Agriculture, the communist Fausto Gullo, implemented a reform program that also redounded to the benefit of the party. The agrarian legislation is too complex to warrant treatment here.[127] It sought, in brief, to provide the impoverished peasantry of the south with land and adequate prices for their products through government subsidies. For tenant farmers and landless laborers, the legislation mandated reforms in the terms of contracts that had kept the southern peasantry subservient to landlords. Significantly, the cooperatives, in which the PCI had considerable influence, were now legally charged with the task of distributing the land. Hence, the peasantry, in the very particular circumstances of the Liberation, found itself encouraged for the first time by a national government to mobilize and to claim the land. In turn, the PCI, as the party of Resistance and of land reform, was able to garner substantial peasant support.

At the end of World War II, then, the PCI had a powerful presence in the workplace, in peasant cooperatives, in working-class and peasant communities, and in the major women's organization. Significantly, the main centers of PCI support were not the intensely proletarian cities of the north, but the more socially diverse areas of the center.[128] As the leading force within the CLN, the party participated in the national government, and would soon exercise important influence in the constitutional assembly and the subsequent national legislatures and in municipal administration.

From this strong, though certainly not uncontested, position, the PCI staked out its claim to contribute to the shaping of the postwar nation. Two expressions encapsulated the strategy Togliatti promoted upon his return to Italy in 1944: *il partito nuovo* (the new party) and *democrazia progressiva* (progressive democracy), and they were interrelated.[129] *Il partito nuovo*, in a substantial departure from a Leninist cadre model, was to be a mass party open to all without prior political investigation. "Progressive democracy"—about which a great deal of confusion reigned—meant that the party would work within the institutions of the democracy to transform the structure of Italian society. The mass party would give to these institutions a "social" content that would over time transform them into institutions of a socialist society. Significantly, the PCI understood democratic institutions to encompass far more than the normal institutions of the state, that is, the parliament, army, state bureaucracy, and municipal administration. The factory, the peasant cooperative, the mass organizations of women, youth, and others were all considered part of the polity and would serve alongside "normal" political institutions in the construction of the new society.

In short, the PCI's strategy granted express political purpose to the institutions of civil society as well as to those of the state. In this broadly conceived political world, the proletariat (or the party) would establish its hegemony—its cultural, social, and political presence that was itself a constitutive part of the revolution. In this manner, the PCI's strategy derived very clearly from major aspects of Gramsci's intellectual approach, notably his view of revolution in the West as a relatively longterm social process entailing the construction of proletarian hegemony.[130]

But it would be a profound mistake to ascribe the innovations of the PCI's strategy solely to the intellectual legacy of Gramsci, to write as if Gramsci's ideas functioned in a historical vacuum—a position adopted by many commentators on the party, whether to damn or to venerate it.[131] The strategic and ideological presumptions articulated by Gramsci and Togliatti had resonance in Italy precisely because of the nature of mass political activism in the Resistance and in the postwar years, which was itself rooted in the contingent events of the war as well as longterm structural features of Italian society. The multifaceted nature of political activism in the Resistance rendered a Leninist-type politics virtually irrelevant. The household, the workplace, and the countryside all proved vital areas of political contestation, and after the liberation, functioned in conjunction with the "normal" spheres of political activity—the ballot box, municipal administration, and national politics. The dictatorship of the proletariat in its specifically Marxist-Leninist sense entailed a politico-military conception of the state—a highly centralized state with massive powers of direction. As Lenin himself came to recognize, the Soviet state at least in part served as the substitute for an undeveloped civil society.[132] In Italy, the economy may have been only partly developed (in comparison with other western European nations), but *civil society was highly developed* as a result of the politics of Resistance, Italy's incomplete and uneven development, and fascist social and economic policies, all of which lent political vitality to such diverse sectors as the workplace, household, and peasant community. A Leninist politics would have meant the suppression of civil society in favor of the centralized state—a position that Togliatti and other PCI leaders were loathe to accept because of their own intellectual orientation and because, for obvious political reasons, they did not want to lose the support so painfully constructed in the Resistance after decades of functioning as a sect on the margins of political life. And if this reasoning did not suffice, Togliatti in particular was well aware of the fact that the western Allies occupied the country, and would hardly have accepted a bolshevized Italy.

Hence, the very broad-based character of political mobilization in Italy reinforced the strategic orientation worked out by Gramsci and Togliatti—as, in turn, the strategy reinforced the determination on the part of the party to function in the broadest range of political space possible.

Yet the strategy encapsulated in the terms "progressive democracy" and "the new party" faced numerous obstacles and was not without inconsistencies. Most seriously, the PCI's strategy of a gradualist transition from capitalism to socialism rested on the presumption that a communist presence would be tolerated both by the nation's conservative elements, notably the industrial elite, landlords, the Church, and large segments of the middle class, and by the British and Americans.[133] In the vain effort to reassure these groups and thereby maintain the Resistance coalition, the PCI leadership reined in some of the more activist elements in the spheres the party dominated, particularly during the years of reconstruction when popular political activism remained at a very high level. The PCI-dominated trade union federation collaborated with employers in the drive to increase production and to rein in the co-management commissions established during the Liberation.[134] Togliatti's notable analysis of civil society as a source of women's oppression marked the closure, not the beginning, of a trenchant reconsideration of gender relations.[135] In the effort to reach an accommodation with Catholic sensibilities, the PCI retreated to a view of the family that, in some respects, did not greatly differ from that of the Christian Democratic Party (DC). The representation of women as determined fighters, characteristic of the Resistance years, soon gave way to depictions of the eternally maternal woman.[136] On abortion the party refused to challenge the Church and the DC. Women's issues in general became subordinated to the more general concerns of peace and reconstruction and the party political conflicts of the Cold War. Increasingly, the UDI became subservient to party direction, and even International Women's Day received scant attention in the party press.[137] And in the countryside the PCI both supported and contained the revived wave of land occupations that engulfed the south in the late 1940s and early 1950s.[138]

Hence, in a situation replete with historical ironies, the party that owed its success to the broad-based political mobilization of the Resistance became hostage to the search for a political party alliance at the apex of society. Progressive democracy and the new party, forged out of the Gramscian intellectual heritage as managed by

Togliatti and the nature of political mobilization in the Resistance, became rationales for holding firm to the party line and maintaining the party's hold on the political space it had already conquered.[139] The PCI's express commitment to *politics* and political alliances led it to undermine the autonomy of the very institutional expressions through which it had become a mass party. The party, so dependent upon popular mobilization, became itself an agent of demobilization.

Conclusion

The three western European communist parties discussed here operated with very different political strategies. Yet their emergence as mass parties reveals some common patterns, and prompts some methodological observations as well.

It is surely significant that the parties under consideration here accomplished their popular breakthroughs in the context of the three great labor-led insurgencies of the first half of the twentieth century—those of the World War I era, the world economic crisis, and the anti-fascist Resistance—which were also the periods of immensely difficult living conditions. In the wake of a generation of scholarship that has challenged any simple and direct connection between material deprivation and popular protest, it becomes necessary to state the obvious: material difficulties do matter. Amid the more recent poststructuralist challenge to the very practice of history, and the effort by some historians to rescue the discipline by redefining the terrain of historical study as exclusively the interpretation of meaning and the organization of knowledge, the point needs to be made: to those who live through the experience, there is a very particular kind of material reality to speedup and unemployment, to hunger and aerial bombardments. Certainly, the heightened militancy of communist parties is largely explained by their emergence, as sects and as mass movements, in the throes of the crises of two world wars and one world-wide depression. The socialist parties, in contrast, emerged more in the context of the longterm structural transformation of European society, which brought with it great difficulties, to be sure, but not the pointedly sharp existential crises that the upheavals of the twentieth century visited upon populations.

Yet it is also true that material deprivation in and of itself hardly suffices as an explanation for the emergence of popular activism and of mass-based communist parties. The three labor-led insurgencies within which the parties achieved their popular breakthroughs erupted in the context also of longterm structural changes in the European political and social economy, which included the rationalization of industrial production, the expansion and then legitimacy crises of state systems, and the heightened politicization of gender.

The process of rationalization that all three nations experienced generated an accumulation of workplace grievances. Workers' sense of exploitation intensified as management forced higher productivity through new technologies and tighter supervision. Wage decreases sometimes accompanied the rationalization drive, and skilled workers in particular suffered from the diminution of their relative autonomy. In Germany in the 1920s (and in Italy in the late 1940s and 1950s), rationalization also resulted in high levels of unemployment.

At the same time, the process of rationalization significantly heightened labor's capacity for mass action. Work forces became somewhat more homogeneous as processes like the assembly line and longwall mining required greater numbers of semi-skilled workers. Yet skilled workers were by no means eliminated from the production process. Rationalization drove, if only temporarily, the skilled and the semi-skilled into a common pool of resentment against new work methods. Skilled workers, with their traditions of workplace autonomy and organizational experience, often served as the driving force of protest, which then stimulated other groups of workers. In addition, rationalization intensified the occupational and geographical concentration of workers—the classic urban-industrial agglomerations of the Ruhr, the Paris Red Belt, and the industrial triangle with Turin at its apex. These concentrations heightened workers' sense of class identification, linked the workplace and the community, and made populations more accessible to political party mobilization. All of these factors were essential preconditions to the eruption of working-class protest and political activism. In Germany, the situation was made more complex by both higher levels of unemployment and the Social Democrats' identification with the Weimar system. In a sense, a second stage of rationalization ensued from the mid-1920s in which the social and political fragmentation of the working class became intermixed.

The chronology of rationalization, it seems to me, thus underlay the sequencing of mass communist party formation. We can roughly date the development of rationalization on a widespread scale in Germany from the turn of the century through the early 1930s (with the partial exception of the inflation years 1914-23); in France from the mid-1920s to the late 1930s; in Italy from the early 1930s into the 1950s (with the exception perhaps of 1943-46). As indicated above, the three parties examined here generally followed this chronology in their breakthrough to popular status. The communist parties as mass parties were formed, then, in large part from both the discontent and the capacity for activism that rationalization generated among workers.

Mass communist parties were also formed in the context of state systems in crisis. In all three cases, central states had assumed greater powers in the course of the twentieth century through the expansion of social welfare programs, internal security forces, and the capacity for warmaking. These trends include the democratic states of Weimar and the Third Republic, which, for example, were not at all shy about exercising repressive measures, often in collaboration with employers, against the radical left, as well as fascist Italy with its effort at total domination of the political sphere. But enhanced state capacities are double-edged. States became more powerful, but they also became the targets of discontent precisely because they assumed so many tasks previously left to civil society or not requiring the mobilization of populations. Warmaking, an extreme but pointed example, may be an effective means of solidifying state power,[140] but only when wars are fought to victorious conclusion. Lost wars may unleash crises of legitimacy, especially in the twentieth century, when effective warmaking is so dependent on popular mobilization. Similarly, social welfare programs that failed to deliver on their promises, as occurred in the Weimar Republic, the late Third Republic, and fascist Italy, only generated hostility to the state systems that were supposed to confer benefits upon their populations.

Hence, the German and Italian communist parties became mass parties in the context of popular revolutions against the Imperial and Fascist states that had lost wars, and then amid the highly contested legitimacy of the successor states. Weimar could not master the crises generated in great part by the impact of World War I. The Badoglio government took a diffident approach to a war that most Italians had, by mid-1943, come to reject, while the Republic of Salò was merely a reconstruction of the fascist regime under German domination. The French case was perhaps less extreme, but the inability of the governments of the Third Republic to resolve the economic crisis, despite the increasing interventionist role of the state, and to eliminate the threat of fascism (real or imagined) undermined their legitimacy. The PCF could capture some of this discontent with the promise of reinvigorating the popular, republican nature of the French state system.

But the legitimacy crises of state systems is not the only crucial dimension of state power. The foregoing study has underscored the critical importance of the local state in the formation of communist parties. The KPD refused to consider the institutions of the local state as anything other than propaganda forums. In large part as a result, its popular base remained highly restricted. In France and in Italy after the war, the local state provided one of the crucial arenas through which the parties broadened the character of their support, especially among women, and implemented the reformist aspects of their strategies. Political power at the local level also had the effect of blunting whatever residual insurrectionary inclinations remained within the two parties—a development with which German communists never really had to contend.

In this regard, the study of communist parties indicates the need for a more highly differentiated analysis of state power. In the North American historical social science literature of the 1980s, and in the neo-Marxist debate that preceded it, the renewed interest in the state turned almost exclusively on the character of the central state. Yet the local state, which plays such a crucial role in the shaping of social movements, is not merely the central state writ small. The political rules vary and the configuration of power can be quite different at the local level.[141]

Furthermore, the character of the local state only underscores the difficulties of classifying state power on any kind of linear scale of weak to strong.[142] Under the Weimar Republic, normally considered a weak state because of its short life span and the numerous political challenges with which it had to contend, the expansion of the state's repressive apparatus and its social welfare activities brought the German working class into ever more direct contact with the state, and decisively shaped working-class political conceptions in both their reformist and radical versions. The local state, however, was very difficult for the KPD to capture because of its own ideological inclinations and because of the federal structure of the German state system, which gave many of the individual state ministries the power to reject locally-elected officials. The Italian state's repressive apparatus expanded dramatically under fascism. But the character of its intervention in other spheres remains highly problematical, and in some senses it emerges "weaker" than Weimar Germany. And in postwar Italy, the effectiveness with which the PCI governed the local state seems to bear little comparison to the fragmented nature of central power. Students of modern France write reflexively of the *étatiste* tradition. Yet in comparison with both Weimar Germany and Fascist Italy, there existed in France a fairly wide diffusion of power to the local level that enabled communists to direct their energies at communal politics. Clearly, state power is not easily subject to quantification, but has to be examined historically and at local, regional, and national levels in terms of the scope and quality of its interventions.

The periods in which the communist parties became mass parties were also characterized by the intensification of women's political activism. The dire material conditions of these periods, which affected women in all of their social roles, fostered their involvement in strikes and demonstrations, food riots and collective petty thievery, community-based social activities and armed resistance. The popular activism of these periods challenged the existing power hierarchies to such an extent that even the organized institutions of opposition like trade unions and political parties were unable to define alone the terms of political protest. In the fluid social circumstances of broad-based popular insurgencies, women were able to assume political roles closed off to them in "normal" times.

The communist parties were, therefore, compelled for practical as well as ideological reasons to come to terms with the political activism of women, a challenge only imperfectly met. The KPD remained most firmly tied to the traditional Marxist view that proletarianization provided the path of liberation for women. As a result, the party concentrated its appeals on women workers and ignored the household as a site of political activism. The PCF came to recognize the political significance of the household, but constructed it as an arena to be protected by the state. Nonetheless, this evolution in strategy, by promoting social reforms at the local and national level, had at least the potential of appealing to all women. The PCI, by lending support to all the varied arenas in which women operated during the Resistance, helped sustain women's activism in a more consistent manner than the other two. As a result, it attracted far greater support from women than was usual for a communist party.

Furthermore, the very activism of women and the emergence of mass-based communist parties that gave at least rhetorical support to the equality of the sexes politicized gender on a more systematic basis than previously. It is hardly accidental that the political debates on the constitutions of the Weimar Republic and the Italian Republic (and the French Fourth Republic, which is beyond the purview of this paper) were preoccupied not only with the forms of political representation, but also with the definition of gender-based roles and the allotment of gender-based rights and responsibilities. Similarly, the Popular Front victory in France placed more conventional political and economic issues in the forefront of the legislative agenda, but also led to an intensified discussion of natalism with all its gender implications and to the ultimate passage, under Daladier, of an extensive family reform act. In addition, both the PCF and the PCI significantly moderated their position on a number of gender-related issues to cement their political alliances and to constitute themselves as mass parties on a reform platform. Most notably, both parties abandoned their commitment to the easy availability of contraceptives and the legalization of abortion. The KPD retained a more radical stance on the abortion issue, but all three parties avoided any kind of sustained critique of power relations within the family. Thus, the specific gender character of their political strategies significantly shaped the constituencies of the communist parties and their mode of insertion into the larger society.

As this last point demonstrates, even communist parties, so fixated on the productive world, developed strategies that related also to the spheres of social reproduction. Each party's politics offered a varying mix of emphases on the workplace, the battlefield, the household, the local state, the streets. Each party's formulation differed, but none operated isolated from the multiple spaces of social life, and none operated in a gender-blind fashion. In this sense, there are at least some lines of continuity between the oppositional politics of the "traditional" labor movement and the new social movements that have emerged since the 1960s. To be sure, the socialist and communist parties sought to subordinate all issues and forms of opposition under the rubric of proletarian hegemony and the teleology of socialist construction. The new social movements, in contrast, tend to celebrate difference and the politics of identity, of ethnicity, race, gender, sexual orientation. In general, they are more attuned to the political saliency of the spheres of reproduction. But to the extent that all social movements in the modern era develop strategies that in some fashion relate to the multiple spheres of social life, there are continuities as well as disjunctures among them, a factor often ignored in the sometimes strident effort to depict the "newness" of the new social movements.[143]

Common, trans-national trends thus underlie the emergence of popular communist parties in Europe. Yet each party also had its particular characteristics. For the parties to achieve mass status, a certain convergence had to emerge between party strategies and specific forms of popular activism, a convergence mediated through the political space within which party and popular activism unfolded. Of course, the Soviet-dominated Comintern played the key role in the formulation of party strategies. But the Comintern could not totally determine the manner in which strategies were implemented,[144] nor determine whether or not a particular strategy would work for a particular party.

The KPD operated in the most restricted political space of the three parties. Driven from the battlefield by the greater firepower of the state and from the workplace by rationalization, the world economic crisis, and employer repression, the party's main sphere of activism became the streets and government agencies. Its militancy, derived from Luxemburg and Lenin, led it to view "normal" political institutions like the Reichstag, the Landtage, and municipal councils as largely platforms for party propaganda. Street battles constituted rehearsals for the ultimate revolutionary combat, so male physical prowess against the police and then the Nazis became the KPD's standard of revolutionary militancy.

By emphasizing physical combativeness, the party won substantial support from some male workers, especially the unemployed. But the idealization of the combative male proletariat as the agent of revolution and the consequent denigration of the household as a terrain of activism sharply limited the KPD's ability to organize among women. Its conventional Marxist belief in the division of society into two essential classes also led it to ignore other social groups. Paeans to the revolutionary potential of the impoverished petty bourgeoisie and peasantry amounted to little more than rhetorical flourishes.

Yet the unemployed, the largest single constituency of the KPD, constituted something of a dilemma for the party. The militancy of their actions, directed against the agencies of the state and the SPD, the party most closely identified with the Republic, accorded with the KPD's militant and insurrectionist strategy derived from Marxism-Leninism. The inconstancy of the unemployed, the swings between apathy and activism, made them difficult to organize on a sustained basis. More importantly, a successful revolution could not be created through street demonstrations and police battles alone. A movement based on the working-class yet isolated from most of the essential institutions of proletarian life—the workplace, the trade unions, the household—could hardly surmount its ultimately marginal status in society. German communism had entered its cul-de-sac even before its bloody repression at the hands of the Nazis.

The shift to the popular front strategy dramatically increased the presence of the PCF within the political spaces of French society. The PCF became a major factor in the trade union federation, the workplace, the national legislature, and numerous municipalities. It could count on a solid working-class base, and its political presence, through which it articulated social issues of broad concern, enabled it at least to begin to attract some support from middle-class elements and women. In this regard, the PCF's shift to pro-natalism proved crucial, as significant as its acceptance of republican institutions, in legitimizing the party. In addition, the PCF had some centers of rural support, though these were not "centers of a hegemonic presence, as [were] the rural bastions of the PCI in central Italy"[145] and rural issues and problems never occupied a central place in PCF strategy in the same way that the "southern question" was of such central significance for the PCI.

Yet the PCF's very accomplishments in the Popular Front (and later the Resistance) enmeshed it in dilemmas that were never totally resolved. The popular front strategy always remained a touchstone for the PCF, one encapsulated in the phrase "party of Villeurbane," the site of its triumphal 1936 congress. The party's inscription into the French political landscape on the basis of republican language, including pronatalism, and the occupation of republican political space ensured that the insurrectionary tendencies of Leninism remained consigned to the *History of the Communist Party of the Soviet Union (Bolshevik), Short Course*, not a truly viable political option. Yet the *Short Course*, with its evocation of the heroic October, was long required reading for party militants. Most seriously, the PCF never theorized the Popular Front into a strategy for the transition to socialism. The Popular Front remained on the level of a tactical approach subject to revision as soon as the contingent political factors themselves changed. As a result, party strategy oscillated between popular front-type alliances and more intransigent, Leninist-type approaches that rejected collaboration with other political groups.

Of the three parties, the PCI came to occupy the widest range of political space. Barred from the "normal" arenas of political activity by the fascist monopolization of power, the party at first could only establish itself in the workplace, which, with the adjacent working-class communities, provided the security in which clandestine activity could develop. With the decision in September 1943 to launch the armed resistance, the PCI quickly became the major force of the partisan war. The very nature of Resistance—the primacy placed on individual initiative and the dependence on the population for support—served to politicize virtually all the arenas of civil society. The PCI's promotion of this broad-based popular insurgency won it support not just from proletarian men, but from other social groups: women and peasants in particular. In the postwar era, the PCI's strong presence in the workplace, the trade unions, peasant cooperatives, municipalities, and the national legislature enabled it to build further on its broad constituency. Viewed in comparison with the Christian Democrats, the PCI's support among women was noticeably weak; viewed cross nationally and in comparison with other communist parties, the PCI was remarkably successful among women.

The PCI's very successful strategy of insertion into society was based not only on the nature of the Resistance. The strategy derived also from a very sophisticated theoretical and political approach invented by Gramsci and further developed by Togliatti, who gave it his own particular turn. While successful in building a mass party, the strategy of progressive democracy made the PCI hostage to alliances with other political groups, the Christian Democratic Party in particular. Progressive democracy became less a strategy for the transition to socialism than a means of securing the party base within society. This entailed the gradual demobilization of popular activism, its channeling into party-directed institutions. Ironically enough, the popular and partly autonomous insurgency of the Resistance, which provided the basis for the PCI's popular breakthrough, had ultimately to be contained and channeled by the party in the futile quest for a political alliance at the apex of society.

The strategies by which the three parties became mass parties and their mode of insertion into the larger society, forged in the crises of the first half of the twentieth century, profoundly shaped their future development. The KPD's construction of a combative mass-based party in the Weimar Republic, the PCF's breakthrough in the Popular Front, the PCI's desperate but successful struggle in the Resistance—these constituted the heroic moments that each party carefully cultivated and inscribed into its culture and politics in the succeeding decades, sharply limiting the ability to undertake new departures. The Leninist-Luxemburgist derived strategy of the KPD, with its hostility to bourgeois institutions and emphasis on democratic centralism and state power, underpinned the Socialist Unity Party's unwavering commitment to strict central direction of the economy and polity—the very policies which created the intractable popular hostility that ultimately proved the undoing of the German Democratic Republic in 1989/90. The ambiguities of the PCF, rooted in its partial insertion into the structures of the nation, help explain its continual oscillation and its inability to move out of the ghetto that was at least in part its own creation. The PCI's achievement of mass status on the basis of diverse and fluid realms of activism and the wartime political coalition help account for its efforts in the 1970s to reach an "historic compromise" with the Christian Democrats, efforts ultimately no more successful than those attempted between 1945 and 1947. Having foregone the insurrectionary path yet unable to establish the historic compromise, the PCI could do little else than accept the realities of its transformation into a democratic party of reform similar to European social democratic parties.

As European communism fades into oblivion and the political divide of the postwar world erodes, it is perhaps appropriate, in conclusion, to examine the ways that division has colored our interpretations of even the pre-1945 period. While a small library of works compare French and Italian communism—with many instructive insights, to be sure—the effacing of German communism, the first mass-based communist party, from the analysis reads back into the history of the first half of the century the division of Europe after World War II.[146] Furthermore, the exclusive focus on Italy and France also promotes a misplaced notion of Latin exceptionalism, and the related idea of a social democratic/Protestant northern Europe and a communist/Catholic south. Even allowing for the rhetorical liberties of a capsule description, this view has a curious conception of the political geography of the continent given the base won by the PCF and the KPD in the northern parts of their countries. Rather than discuss the peculiarities of southern Europe,[147] or the singularity of French patterns,[148] or Germany's unique, conflict-ridden road to modernity,[149] it seems more fruitful to understand the emergence of popular western European communism as a history, to steal a phrase from Togliatti, of unity in diversity: as a common, integral part of the classic epoch of working-class representation—an historical epoch that has now been superseded—but with particular characteristics arising out of the national patterns of political economy, popular activism, and party strategies.

Notes

1. See, for example, André Gorz, *Farewell to the Working Class: An Essay on Post-Industrial Socialism* (London, 1982); Martin Jacques and Francis Mulhern, eds. *The Forward March of Labour Halted?* (London: Verso, 1982); Rolf Ebbighausen and Friedrich Tiemann, eds., *Das Ende der Arbeiterbewegung in Deutschland? Ein Diskussionsband zum sechzigsten Geburtstag von Theo Pirker* (Opladen: Westdeutscher Verlag, 1984); and Geoff Eley, "Labor History, Social History, Alltagsgeschichte: Experience, Culture, and the Politics of the Everyday—A New Direction for German Social History?," *Journal of Modern History* 61:2 (June 1989): 297-343, who specifically links the emergence of *Alltagsgeschichte* in Germany with the decline of the traditional labor movement.

2. Leaving aside the Spanish Communist Party and the very particular circumstances of its emergence and then suppression.

3. Early examples, which established the interpretive framework for decades, are Franz Borkenau, *World Communism: A History of the Communist International* (New York: Norton, 1939) and Ruth Fischer, *Stalin and German Communism* (1948; New Brunswick: Transaction Books, 1982). See also the standard Comintern histories of Milorad M. Drachkovitch and Branko Lazitch, eds. *The Comintern: Historical Highlights* (New York: Praeger, 1966); Julius Braunthal, *History of the International*, vol. 2: *1914-1943* (New York: Praeger, 1967); Helmut Gruber, *Soviet Russia Masters the Comintern: International Communism in the Era of Stalin's Ascendancy* (New York: Anchor Books, 1974); and Fernando Claudin, *The Communist Movement: From Comintern to Cominform* (New York: Monthly Review Press, 1975). For the individual parties, the writings of Hermann Weber on the KPD and of Annie Kriegel on the PCF are prototypical. Both are highly prolific authors whose work constitutes the intellectual and empirical reference point for all subsequent studies of the parties. Both are certainly attuned to the national dimensions of communist party histories. Yet ultimately, their explanations for the historical development of, respectively, the KPD and the PCF are situated in terms of decisions and developments made in Moscow. For representative works, see Hermann Weber, *Die Wandlung des deutschen Kommunismus: Die Stalinisierung der KPD in der Weimarer Republik*, 2 vols. (Frankfurt a.M.: Europäische Verlagsanstalt, 1969); Weber, *Kommunistische Bewegung und realsozialistischer Staat: Beiträge zum deutschen und internationalen Kommunismus. Hermann Weber zum 60. Geburtstag*, ed. Werner Müller (Cologne: Bund-Verlag, 1988); Weber, *Aufbau und Fall einer Diktatur: Kritischen Beiträge zur Geschichte der DDR* (Cologne: Bund-Verlag, 1991); Annie Kriegel, *Aux Origines du communisme français 1914-1920*, 2 vols. (Paris: Mouton, 1964); Kriegel, "Les Communistes français et la question du pouvoir (1920-1939)," *Annales: économies, sociétés, civilisations* 21:6 (November-December 1966): 1245-58;

Kriegel, *Les Communistes français dans leur premier demi siècle 1920-1970*, 2nd ed. (Paris: Editions du Seuil, 1985). The historiography on the Italian party is different, largely because it has developed within the PCI and its exponents have had a political as well as an historical interest in exploring the national dimension of Italian communism. But even this historiography has been largely political in nature, and only in recent years have social histories become more prominent. The major study is, of course, Paolo Spriano, *Storia del Partito comunista italiano*, 5 vols. (Turin: Einaudi, 1967-75).

4. The publication of the archives of Angelo Tasca, the Italian Communist Party's representative to the Comintern from 1928 to 1930, and of Jules Humbert-Droz, the head of the Latin Secretariat for much of the 1920s, has been especially important in this regard, as has the availability of the PCI archives and, in a more restricted fashion, the PCF archives. Much more stands to be learned in the next few years as the KPD archives and, more hesitantly, the Comintern archives in Moscow become open to scholars. See Istituto Giangiacomo Feltrinelli, *Annali* 11 (1966) and 14 (1969) for the Tasca archives, and *Archives de Jules Humbert-Droz*, 3 vols., ed. Institute for Social History (Dordrecht: D. Reidel, 1970).

5. References to particular works are provided below in the sections on each of the parties.

6. This point about the lack of attention in recent studies to the international dimension has also been made by Geoff Eley, "International Communism in the Heyday of Stalin," *New Left Review* 157 (May/June 1986): 90-100; Geoff Eley and Ronald Suny, "University of Michigan Project on International Communism," *International Labor and Working Class History* 30 (Fall 1986): 103-107; and, from a very different vantage point, Tony Judt, "'The Spreading Notion of the Town': Some Recent Writings on French and Italian Communism," *Historical Journal* 28:4 (December 1985): 1011-1021.

7. My use of political space is influenced by the notion of "political opportunity structure" developed in American political science, and by human geographers' and sociologists' understanding of space. On my reading, however, "political opportunity structure" does not leave enough room for the *creation* of political space by historical actors--even though some of the formulators of the notion are deeply attuned, in their own empirical work, to the agency of popular movements. On the concept see especially Sidney Tarrow, *Struggle, Politics, and Reform: Collective Action, Social Movements, and Cycles of Protest*, Cornell Studies in International Affairs: Western Societies Program Occasional Paper No. 21 (Ithaca: Cornell University Center for International Studies, 1989), and for a very fruitful application, idem., *Democracy and Disorder: Protest and Politics in Italy, 1965-1975* (Oxford: Clarendon Press, 1989). For a different but related application, Sara M. Evans and Harry C. Boyte, *Free Spaces: The Sources of Democratic Change in America* (New York: Harper & Row, 1986). See also the discussion of place as the point of mediation between structure and agency in John A. Agnew, *Place and Politics: The Geographical Mediation of State*

and Society (Boston: Allen & Unwin, 1987), as well other theoretical and empirical studies that explore the relationship between collective action and spatial location: Eric Sheppard and Trevor J. Barnes, *The Capitalist Space Economy: Geographical Analysis after Ricardo, Marx and Sfarra* (London: Unwin Hyman, 1990), pp. 199-261; David Harvey, *Consciousness and the Urban Experience: Studies in the History and Theory of Capitalist Urbanization* (Baltimore: Johns Hopkins University Press, 1985), esp. pp. 36-62, who draws somewhat too sharp a distinction between workplace and community-based action; Allan Pred, *Place, Practice and Structure: Social and Spatial Transformation in Southern Sweden, 1750-1850* (Totowa, New Jersey: Barnes & Noble Books, 1986), pp. 5-31; Andrew Kirby, "Time, Space and Collective Action: Political Space/Political Geography," (ms., 1989); and Anthony Giddens, *The Constitution of Society: Outline of the Theory of Structuration* (Berkeley and Los Angeles: University of California Press, 1984). I am not certain, however, that any of the individuals cited here would recognize or find congenial my appropriation of their work.

8. See Anthony Giddens, *Central Problems in Social Theory: Action, Structure and Contradiction in Social Analysis* (Berkeley and Los Angeles: University of California Press, 1979) and *The Constitution of Society*, and the recent critique by William H. Sewell, Jr., which decisively moves forward the discussion on structure and agency: "A Theory of Structure: Duality, Agency, and Transformation," *American Journal of Sociology* 98:1 (July 1992): 1-29.

9. The major study on the KPD remains Hermann Weber, *Die Wandlung des deutschen Kommunismus: Die Stalinisierung der KPD in der Weimarer Republik*, 2 vols. (Frankfurt a. M.: Europäische Verlagsanstalt, 1969).

10. Even many so-called "rightists" and "reconcilers" in the party had behind them actual experience in armed revolutionary combat, and actively promulgated revolutionary politics. Ernst Meyer, for example, was quoted by governmental authorities in 1926, i.e., during the KPD's and Comintern's "moderate" phase, as writing: "Also today the Communist Party raises against the pacifistic and weak social democratic slogan, 'Never again war!' the single real revolutionary slogan: *'Civil war against imperialist war!'*" (Reichskommissar für Überwachung der öffentlichen Ordnung an Reichsminister des Innern, 10 August 1926, Bundesarchiv Koblenz R43 I/2673, Bl. 169.)

11. Luxemburg's democratic ideals, including the renowned pronouncements against the authoritarian aspects of the Bolshevik Revolution, proved in succeeding years highly problematic for the party and the Comintern. The effort to revise posthumously her views involved even her closest friends and associates, e.g. Clara Zetkin, *Um Rosa Luxemburgs Stellung zur russischen Revolution* (Hamburg: Verlag Carl Hoym Nachf., 1922).

12. Or to put it differently (and anachronistically), "democracy is in the streets."

13. See the justly renowned tract, "The Mass Strike, the Political Party and the Trade Unions" in *Rosa Luxemburg Speaks*, ed. Mary-Alice Waters (New York: Pathfinder Press, 1970), pp. 153-218 and esp. pp. 181-82.

14. The founding conference of the KPD was one of the few instances when she did sketch out the future political order. See Hermann Weber, ed., *Der Gründungsparteitag der KPD: Protokoll und Materialien* (Frankfurt a.M.: Europäische Verslagsanstalt, 1969) and Rosa Luxemburg, *Gesammelte Werke*, vol. 4, ed. Institut für Marxismus-Leninismus beim ZK der SED (Berlin: Dietz Verlag, 1974), pp. 442-52 and 481-513.

15. Her contributions to the mass strike debate prior to World War I are perhaps the best-known example of her enthrallment with popular activism. See "The Mass Strike, the Political Party and the Trade Unions," in *Rosa Luxemburg Speaks*, pp. 153-218. But note also that in her *Gesammelte Werke*, vols. 2-4, ed. Institut für Marxismus-Leninismus beim ZK der SED (Berlin: Dietz Verlag, 1972-74) and in *Rote Fahne*, the KPD daily, under her editorship, the emphasis is on strategy and tactics and contemporary events rather than extended theoretical analyses. In this regard, as in so many others, Luxemburg straddled the sensibilities of the Second and Third Internationals. Leszek Kolakowski misinterprets Luxemburg, I think, by exaggerating the deterministic element in her thought. In her theoretical writings she sought to prove the historical inevitabiliy of capitalism's collapse, but this did not at all deter her from promoting a voluntaristic politics. Like many Marxists, Luxemburg presents an unresolved tension between voluntarism and necessity. See Kolakowski's comments in *Main Currents of Marxism*, vol. 2: *The Golden Age* (Oxford: Oxford University Press, 1978), esp. pp. 75-97. Peter Nettl, in his magisterial biography, *Rosa Luxemburg*, abridged ed. (Oxford: Oxford University Press, 1969), is a bit too uncritical of his subject.

16. "Dem Feind den Daumen aufs Auge, das Knie auf die Brust!" *Ruhr-Echo* 29 March 1921. The headline and article were scheduled to appear in *Rote Fahne*, the main party daily, but the entire issue was seized by the authorities.

17. *Rote Fahne* 14 April 1921. After a period of reflection, the Comintern became more critical of the KPD's actions.

18. And they were so honored down to the very end of the German Democratic Republic. See the text and pictures of the yearly commemorative ceremonies at the Leuna plant in *Geschichte der VEB Leuna-Werke 'Walter Ulbricht' 1916 bis 1945* ed. Kreisleitung der SED des VEB Leuna-Werke 'Walter Ulbricht' (Leuna, 1989), pp. 1-8.

19. See Diane P. Koenker, William G. Rosenberg, and Ronald Grigor Suny, eds., *Party, State, and Society in the Russian Civil War: Explorations in Social History* (Bloomington: Indiana University Press, 1989), especially the essay by Sheila Fitzpatrick, "The Legacy of the Civil War," pp. 385-98.

20. See Kurt G.P. Schuster, *Der Rote Frontkämpferbund 1924-1929: Beiträge zur Geschichte und Organisationsstruktur eines politischen Kampfbundes* (Düsseldorf: Droste Verlag, 1975). The memoirs of Erich

Wollenberg (typescript, Hoover Institution Archives), who was active in various revolutionary efforts and in the KPD's clandestine military apparatus, are quite illuminating on the military activities and ethos of party militants in the 1920s.

21. These impressions are based on reading the *Arbeiter-Illustrierte-Zeitung* (hereafter *AIZ*) from 1926 to 1932. Some especially revealing photos can be found in the following issues (the paper variously used volume and issue numbers, dates, or a combination of the two): 10 (1926), 5 June 1927, 19 June 1927, 25 April 1928, 9 May 1928 (the photo of Thälmann), 4 (1930), 31 (1930), 49 (1931), 24 (1932).

22. On the KPD's absorption of aspects of Nazi rhetoric and practice, see most recently the comments of Thomas Childers, "The Social Language of Politics in Germany: The Sociology of Political Discourse in the Weimar Republic," *American Historical Review* 95:2 (April 1990): 350-51, and Conan Fischer, *The German Communists and the Rise of Nazism* (New York: St. Martin's Press, 1991). Fischer demonstrates far more systematically than anyone previously the many points of contact between the NSDAP and KPD. But the result is a somewhat distorted picture of the KPD, one that overemphasizes its nationalistic orientation and neglects the centrality of class in the KPD's ideology and strategy.

23. See Eve Rosenhaft, *Beating the Fascists? The German Communists and Political Violence, 1929-1933* (Cambridge: Cambridge University Press, 1983) and "Working-Class Life and Working-Class Politics: Communists, Nazis and the State in the Battle for the Streets, Berlin 1928-1932," in Richard Bessel and E.J. Feuchtwanger, eds. *Social Change and Political Development in Weimar Germany* (London: Croom Helm, 1981), pp. 207-40.

24. *AIZ*, 1926-32. Some particularly striking examples are in the following issues: 12 (1926), 15 (1926), 31 January 1928, 18 April 1928, 16 (1930)

25. On this issue generally see Silvia Kontos, *Die Partei kämpft wie ein Mann: Frauenpolitik der KPD in der Weimarer Republik* (Frankfurt a. M.: Verlag Roter Stern, 1979). The KPD's position here followed the Comintern's guidelines on organizing women, which were drafted by Clara Zetkin and were published in Zetkin, "Richtlinien für die Kommunistische Frauenbewegung," *Kommunistische Internationale* 3:15 (1921): 530-55. Extensive excerpts and commentary are provided by Karin Bauer, *Clara Zetkin und die proletarische Frauenbewegung* (Berlin: Oberbaum Verlag, 1978), pp. 172-84. In general on the Comintern and women, see Aurelia Camparini, *Questione femminile e Terza internazionale* (Bari: De Donato, 1978).

26. On women in the labor force, all of which underscore the rather minimal increase in women's labor participation rates despite the intense public discussion, see Richard Bessel "'Eine nicht allzu große Beunruhigung des Arbeitsmarktes': Frauenarbeit und Demobilmachung in Deutschland nach dem Ersten Weltkrieg," *Geschichte und Gesellschaft* 9:2 (1983): 211-29; Renate Bridenthal and Claudia Koonz, "Beyond *Kinder, Küche, Kirche*:

Weimar Women in Politics and Work," in Renate Bridenthal, Atina Grossmann, and Marion Kaplan, eds., *When Biology Became Destiny: Women in Weimar and Nazi Germany* (New York: Monthly Review Press, 1984), pp. 44-53; G. Wellner, "Industriearbeiterinnen in der Weimarer Republik: Arbeitsmarkt, Arbeit und Privatleben 1919-1933," *Geschichte und Gesellschaft* 7 (1981): 534-54; and Tim Mason, "Women in Germany, 1925-1940: Family, Welfare and Work," 2 parts *History Workshop* 1 (1978): 74-111 and 2 (1978): 5-32.

27. Hans-Jürgen Arendt, "Weibliche Mitglieder der KPD in der Weimarer Republik: Zahlenmäßige Stärke und soziale Stellung," *Beiträge zur Geschichte der Arbeiterbewegung* 19 (1977), p. 654. Arendt provides the most thorough account, though many of the figures are estimates, as he points out. Despite the low percentage, the KPD in this period had the highest proportion of female membership of any of the communist parties in the developed countries.

28. Gabriele Bremme, *Die politische Rolle der Frau in Deutschland: Eine Untersuchung über den Einfluß der Frauen bei Wahlen und ihre Teilnahme in Partei und Parlament* (Göttingen: Vandenhoeck & Ruprecht, 1956), pp. 73-74.

29. See, for example, *AIZ* 4 April 1928, p. 7. The campaign for "rationalized" households cut through the political divisions of the Weimar period, as Mary Nolan shows (though she does not discuss the KPD): "'Housework made Easy': The Taylorized Housewife in Weimar Germany's Rationalized Economy," *Feminist Studies* 16:3 (Fall 1990): 549-73.

30. Bridenthal and Koonz, "Beyond *Kinder, Küche, Kirche*," p. 58, n. 29.

31. *AIZ*, 10 August 1927, p. 12 and 8:12 (1929), pp. 4-5.

32. Atina Grossmann, "Abortion and Economic Crisis: The 1931 Campaign Against Paragraph 218," in Bridenthal, Grossmann, and Kaplan, eds. *When Biology Became Destiny*, pp. 66-86.

33. Kontos, *Die Partei kämpft wie ein Mann*. The memoirs of Erich Wollenberg, cited above, are also revealing in this regard. Aside from a few prominent leaders like Ruth Fischer and her mother and sister, the only women that appear in a nearly eight-hundred page typescript are a few dimly-depicted wives of male comrades who provide Wollenberg with shelter and a meal while he is hiding out from the police.

34. Ironically, the one instance in which a general strike did occur—against the Kapp-Putsch in 1920—the KPD hesitated and only belatedly joined the movement.

35. See *Kämpfendes Leuna: Die Geschichte des Kampfes der Leuna Arbeiter*, Teil I, 1. Halbband (1916-1933) (Berlin: Verlag Tribüne, 1961). Workers' efforts to undermine piecework rates by claiming pay for work they did not do or by manipulating their work time to their own advantage aroused the intense ire of management, and was one of the prime factors leading to heightened control over the labor force. Foremen came under particular

criticism for not overseeing carefully enough the workers under their direction. Particularly revealing is: " Rundschreiben Nr. 29, Abteilung für Arbeiterangelegenheiten an sämtlicher Herren Betriebsführer," 4 April 1922, Betriebsarchiv der Leuna-Werke (hereafter BLW) 1321.

36. See especially Lore Heer-Kleinert, *Die Gewerkschaftspolitik der KPD in der Weimarer Republik* (Frankfurt a.m: Campus Verlag, 1983) and Werner Müller, *Lohnkampf, Massenstreik, Sowjetmacht: Ziele und Grenzen der "Revolutionären Gewerkschafts-Opposition" (RGO) in Deutschland 1928 bis 1933* (Cologne: Bund-Verlag, 1988). It should be noted also that the communist rank and file was no less hostile to the unions than the leadership. During the KPD's "moderate" periods, as in 1926 and 1927, the leadership had to exert great efforts, often with only limited success, to convince the members that it was their responsibility to join the existing unions. See, for example, the report of an instructor sent by the Central Committee to the regional organization in the Ruhr in 1927, "Bericht über die Reise nach dem Ruhrgebiet am 17. März 1927," [unsigned] Institut für Geschichte der Arbeiterbewegung, Zentrales Parteiarchiv I 3/18-19/13, Bl. 1-2.

37. For a further development of this argument, see Rosenhaft, *Beating the Fascists?* and Eric D. Weitz, "State Power, Class Fragmentation, and the Shaping of German Communist Politics, 1890-1933," *Journal of Modern History* 62:2 (June 1990): 279-93. See also Siegfried Bahne, "Die Erwerbslosenpolitik der KPD in der Weimarer Republik," in Hans Mommsen and Winfried Schulze, eds., *Vom Elend der Handarbeit: Probleme historischer Unterschichtenforschung* (Stuttgart: Klett-Cotta, 1981), pp. 477-96.

38. Detlev Peukert, "The Lost Generation: Youth Unemployment and the End of the Weimar Republic," in Richard J. Evans and Dick Geary, eds., *The German Unemployed: Experiences and Consequences of Mass Unemployment from the Weimar Republic to the Third Reich* (London: Croom Helm, 1987), pp. 261-80 and Peter D. Stachura, *The Weimar Republic and the Younger Proletariat: An Economic and Social Analysis* (New York: St. Martin's Press, 1989), esp. pp. 94-132. But for some evidence that cautions against overlooking the unemployment of older workers, see Weitz, "State Power, Class Fragmentation, and the Shaping of German Communist Politics," pp. 289-91. Authoritative on labor in the second half of the Weimar Republic are the two volumes by Heinrich August Winkler, *Der Schein der Normalität* and *Der Weg in die Katastrophe* (Berlin: Dietz, 1985 and 1987).

39. See the fragment of a letter from the Leuna-Werke to Herrn Ersten Amtsanwalt, Amtsgericht Halle, 24 December 1924, BLW 1327; "Jahresbericht der Werksaufsicht für das Jahr 1924," BLW 1326, Bl. 13 (of report); "Jahresbericht der Werksaufsicht für das Jahr 1925," BLW 1330, Bl.14-15 (of report); "Jahresbericht der Werksaufsicht für das Jahr 1926," BLW 1332, Bl. 15-16 (of report), "Jahresbericht der Werksaufsicht für das Jahr 1927," BLW 1327, Bl. 17-18 (of report).

40. Eva Cornelia Schöck, *Arbeitslosigkeit und Rationalisierung: Die Lage der Arbeiter und die kommunistische Gewerkschaftspolitik 1920-1928* (Frankfurt a.M.: Campus Verlag, 1977), p. 113. For other evidence along these lines, see Weitz, "State Power, Class Fragmentation, and the Shaping of German Communist Politics," pp. 288-89.

41. Arnedt, "Weibliche Mitglieder der KPD," pp. 657-58. Among female members, the percentage was even lower. Of the employed members in 1929, only 6 percent were women.

42. See the party and Comintern statistics in Wienand Kaasch, "Die soziale Struktur der KPD," *Kommunistische Internationale* 9:19 (1928): 1057-58 and O. Pjatnitzki, "Die Errungenschaften, die Mängel und die nächsten Aufgaben der Organisationsarbeit der KI-Sektionen," *Kommunistische Internationale* 8:17 (April 1927): 820-30; 8:18 (May 1927): 879-91; 8:19 (May 1927): 928-33. Party members were themselves sometimes reluctant to organize cells because they feared employer retaliation or because they were loathe to engage in the intense campaign against the unions and the SPD that often constituted the primary activity of a cell.

43. Rosenhaft, *Beating the Fascists?* and Weitz, "State Power, Class Fragmentation, and the Shaping of German Communist Politics," for the development of this argument.

44. Cited in Weber, *Die Wandlung*, vol. 1, p. 334. Weber provides some other choice examples: Hermann Remmele, "This is a nice stall here!"; Werner Scholem, "The government of this racketeer Republic!" The delegation came equipped with pipes and whistles, which it used frequently to express its displeasure. A good study of the KPD Reichstag and Landtage delegations remains to be written. More satsifactory work has been published, for once, on the municipal level.

45. See the documents in Stadtarchiv Essen Rep. 102 Abt. I 337: Prussian Minister of the Interior to Regierungspräsident Düsseldorf, 4 June 1924; Regierungpräsident Düsseldorf to Landräte, et. al., 14 June 1924; "Auszug aus dem Protokoll des Verfassungsausschuß [of Essen Stadtverordnetenversammlung]," 20 and 26 June 1924; Regierungspräsident Düsseldorf to Oberbürgermeistern, et. al., 21 June 1924; "Auszug aus dem Beschlussbüche der Stadtverordnetenversammlung in Essen, 27 June 1924. The scene was repeated in municipal councils throughout Germany. Ultimately, the party leadership was forced to recognize the foolishness of the action, and ordered elected members to take the oath of office.

46. Georg Fülberth, *Die Beziehungen zwischen SPD und KPD in der Kommunalpolitik der Weimarer Periode 1918/19 bis 1933* (Cologne: Pahl-Rugenstein, 1985), p. 69, whose point, however, is a bit different. In general, Fülberth and Beatrix Herlemann, *Kommunalpolitik der KPD im Ruhrgebiet 1924-1933* (Wuppertal: Peter Hammer Verlag, 1977), take a somewhat more positive view than I would of the KPD's involvement in representative institutions.

47. The KPD's own guidelines for parliamentary work stated:

When communists participate in elections and in the activities of the
parliaments, it is to use the tribune of parliament for revolutionary
enlightenment of the working class, for unmasking the bourgeois
parties and Social Democracy and the capitalist class character of
parliament...In addition, communists use parliament to represent the
interests of all working people against the exploitation of monopoly
capitalist industry and agriculture.

Cited in Weber, *Die Wandlung*, vol. 1, p. 340. Weber argues, however, that
in reality communists at times took a more constructive and practical
approach to parliamentary work than the party's own guidelines
recommended. My estimation is somewhat more negative.

48. Fülberth, *Die Beziehungen zwischen SPD und KPD in der
Kommunal*, pp. 115-16 and Andreas Dorpalen, "SPD und KPD in der
Endphase der Weimarer Republik," *Vierteljahreshefte für Zeitgeschichte* 31:1
(January 1983): 84 note 28.

49. Wienand Kaasch, "Die soziale Struktur der KPD," *Kommunistische
Internationale* 9:19 (1928): 1051-52. It is interesting to note that party
members identified themselves by trade even when unemployed, indicating
their continual self-identification as workers.

50. See Jürgen W. Falter, "Unemployment and the Radicalisation of the
German Electorate, 1928-1933: An Aggregate Data Analysis with Special
Emphasis on the Rise of National Socialism," in Peter D. Stachura, ed.,
Unemployment and the Great Depression in Germany (London: Macmillan,
1986), pp. 187-208, who shows that a correlation exists between areas of
high unemployment and KPD support. The same does not hold for the
NSDAP.

51. On the PCF in this period, see Philippe Robrieux, *Histoire intérieure
du Parti communiste*, vol. 1: *1920-1945* (Paris: Fayard, 1980), among many
others. Albert Vassart, memoirs (typescript, Hoover Institution Archives)
and Henri Barbé, "Souvenirs de militant et de dirigeant communiste,"
(typescript, Hoover Institution Archives) are informative and illuminating on
the PCF in the early 1930s, but both are subject to the selectivity of so many
memoirs by former communists.

52. The most generous, and probably exaggerated, estimate is that in the
interwar period the proletariat constituted around 43 percent of the
population. See Alfred Sauvy, *Histoire économique de la France entre les
deux guerres*, vol. 2 (Paris: Ed. Economica, 1984), p. 38.

On Comintern policies in this period, see Eric D. Weitz, "Bukharin and
'Bukharinism' in the Comintern, 1919-1929," in Nicholas N. Kozlov and
Eric D. Weitz, eds., *Nikolai Ivanovich Bukharin: A Centenary Appraisal*
(New York: Praeger, 1990), pp. 59-91. Jules Humbert-Droz, the head of the
Comintern's Latin Secretariat, proudly claims the term "class against class"
as his own invention: *De Lénine à Staline: Dix Ans au Service de*

l'Internationale communiste 1921-1931. Memoires de Jules Humbert-Droz, vol. 2 (Neuchâtel: Editions de la Baconnière, 1971), pp. 277-82.

53. In the Paris suburb of Ivry, for example, the PCF grew steadily through the 1920s and 1930s, and held on to the municipality from 1925 onwards. But in Bagneux, a different kind of suburb, class against class severely limited the impact of the local PCF group, which nevertheless did gain important experience in this period. See Bernard Chambaz, "L'implantation du Parti communiste française à Ivry," in Jacques Girault, ed., *Sur L'implantation du Parti communiste française dans l'entre deux guerres* (Paris: Editions sociales, 1977), pp. 147-77 and Annie Fourcaut, "L'implantation du Parti communiste dans un groupe d'HBM: La Cité du Cahmp des Oiseaux à Bagneux (1932-1935)," in *idem.*, pp. 179-203. On the PCF in the Nord, see M.I. Yannakakis, "Le P.C.F. dans la région du Nord (1920-1936)," including the discussion that follows, *Revue du Nord* 221 (April-June 1974): 239-45. In a number of communes in the Nord the PCF grew steadily throughout the interwar period, seemingly irrespective of the particular strategies. However, Marcel Gillet, "L'évolution du Parti communiste de 1921 à 1934 dan la région Nord-Pas-de-Calais," *Revue du Nord* 221 (April-June 1974): 233-38, sees the PCF as isolated in the region until the Popular Front period.

54. There is no need to go into detail here about the political process by which the Comintern and the PCF adopted the new strategy. It will suffice to point out that the most recent research has demonstrated that the new strategy derived from initiatives begun by both Comintern leaders in Moscow and the PCF itself, and that Stalin acquiesced to the reversal primarily because of the strategic interests of the Soviet Union, which impelled him to seek alliances with the western democracies against National Socialist Germany. The demise of the KPD following the Nazi rise to power meant the loss of the largest Comintern party outside of the Soviet Union and the leading exponent of the third period strategy, and made clear the need for a strategy more attuned to the real-life circumstances of western societies. Whether out of clear-sighted political concerns or fear for his own position, Thorez recognized the need for a strategy more in accord with the realities of French politics and French society, and he found support especially among those party militants engaged in practical work, such as Benôit Frachon, the Politburo member in charge of trade union work, Renaud Jean, the leading spokesman on peasant matters, and PCF elected officials in the municipalities. The success of Jacques Doriot in St.-Denis, one of the "practicals" and an early advocate of unity of action with the SFIO, provided added impetus to the change in strategy. For some of the recent studies see Roger Martelli, "Une introduction à l'année 1934: Le PCF, l'Internationale et la France," *Cahiers d'histoire de l'Institut Maurice Thorez* 18 (1984): 5-23; E.H. Carr, *Twilight of the Comintern 1930-1935* (New York: Pantheon, 1982), pp. 184-207; John Santore, "The Comintern's United Front Initiative of May 1934: French or Soviet Inspiration?" *Canadian Journal of History* 16 (December 1981): 405-23; Jonathan Haslam, "The Comintern and the Origins of the Popular Front, 1934-1935," *Historical Journal* 25:3 (September 1979):

673-91. For the traditional view that the entire development originated in Moscow, see Célie Vassart and Albert Vassart, "The Moscow Origins of the French 'Popular Front,'" in Drachkovitch and Lazitch, *The Comintern: Historical Highlights*, pp. 234-52. Julian Jackson, *The Popular Front in France: Defending Democracy, 1934-1938* (Cambridge: Cambridge University Press, 1988), pp. 32-36, provides the most recent synthesis of the scholarship, though by arguing in support of the Vassarts' account, he contradicts his later statement that the Popular Front was a result of the interaction among domestic French politics, debates in the Comintern, and a new orientation in Soviet foreign policy, though the decision was ultimately made in Moscow. In the Vassarts' account, little weight is given to the impact of domestic French developments. Philippe Burrin, "Diplomatie soviétique, Internationale communiste et PCF au tournant du Front populaire (1934-35)," *Relations internationales* 45 (Spring 1986): 19-34, departs from most recent analyses by restating the predominant role of the Soviet Union and of Stalin personally in the shift to the Popular Front.

55. Jackson, *The Popular Front*, provides the best synthesis. I have relied also on the essays in Pierre Renouvin and Réné Rémond, eds., *Léon Blum: Chef de Gouvernement 1936-1937*, 2nd ed. (Paris: Presses de la Fondation Nationale des Sciences Politiques, 1981) especially Jean Touchard and Louis Bodin, "L'État de l'opinion au début de l'année 1936," pp. 49-68 and Antoine Prost, "Les Grèves de Juin 1936: Essai d'interprétation," pp. 69-87. On the formulation of the Popular Front program, see Julian Jackson, *The Politics of Depression in France, 1932-1936* (Cambridge: Cambridge University Press, 1985), pp. 112-33.

56. See Tony Judt, *Marxism and the French Left: Studies in Labour and Politics in France, 1830-1981* (Oxford: Clarendon Press, 1986), esp. pp. 243-47.

57. Jackson, *Popular Front*, pp. 39, 319 fn. 47; Tyler Stovall, "French Communism and Suburban Development: The Rise of the Paris Red Belt," *Journal of Contemporary History* 24:3 (July 1989): 452.

58. Tyler Stovall, "'Friends, Neigbors, and Communists': Community Formation in Suburban Paris during the early Twentieth Century," *Journal of Social History* 22:2 (Winter 1988): 237-54; "French Communists and Suburban Development;" and *The Rise of the Paris Red Belt* (Berkeley and Los Angeles: University of California Press, 1990). See also Annie Fourcaut, *Bobigny, Banlieue Rouge* (Paris: Éditions Ouvrières Presses de la Fondation Nationale des Sciences Politiques, 1986). For examples from other communities, see Fourcaut, "L'Implantation du Parti communiste dans un groupe d'HBM" and "La conquête d'une municipalité par le P.C.F. au moment du Front populaire: Les élections municipales de 1935 à Bagneux. Sur la validité d'une monographie communale," *Cahiers d'histoire de l'Institut Maurice Thorez* 19 (1976): 93-103 and Chambaz, "L'implantation du Parti communiste à Ivry." The PCF's popular weekly *Regards* ran a multi-part series in the summer of 1935—i.e., after the Popular Front's victory in the municipal elections—that highlighted the social and cultural

achievements of the communes it controlled. A great deal of space was devoted to the vacation colonies in the countryside. See the series "La Ceinture rouge," 30 May 1935-15 August 1935.

59. Stovall, "'Friends, Neighbors, and Communists,'" p. 249.

60. For some examples see Stovall, "French Communism and Suburban Development," pp. 445, 452 and Fourcaut, *Bobigny*, pp. 169-72.

61. Fourcaut, *Bobigny*, pp. 169-72.

62. See "Rapport de la Section féminine du P.C.F." in Danielle Tartakowsky, "Le P.C.F. et les femmes (1926)," *Cahiers d'histoire de l'Institut Maurice Thorez* 14 (1975), esp. pp. 200-02, 206. Significantly, the PCF periodical directed at women was entitled *L'Ouvrière*. Also, in explaining the tasks of the party's women's commissions, the leadership called upon them to detail the conditions of exploitation in the workplace; not a word was offered about conditions in the household and of family life.

63. On this issue generally see François Delpla, "Les Communistes français et la sexualité (1932-1938)," *Mouvement social* 91 (1975): 121-52 and William H. Schneider, "The Eugenics Movement in France, 1890-1940," in Mark B. Adams, ed. *The Wellborn Science: Eugenics in Germany, France, Brazil, and Russia* (New York: Oxford University Press, 1990), pp. 97-102.

64. Cited in Schneider, "The Eugenics Movement in France," p. 99.

65. Cited in Siân Reynolds, "Women, Men and the 1936 Strikes in France," in Martin S. Alexander and Helen Graham, eds., *The French and Spanish Popular Fronts: Comparative Perspectives* (Cambridge: Cambridge University Press, 1989), p. 199.

66. Cited in Delpla, "Les Communistes français et la sexualité," p. 141.

67. *Regards* 30 May 1935, 21 May 1936, 20 May 1937, 19 August 1937.

68. Delpla, "Les Communistes français et la sexualité," p. 146.

69. For example, *Regards*, 17 December 1937, pp. 20-21, in which the women's column carried the headlines "Pour vôtre santé" and "Pour vôtre beauté" and displayed pictures of babies in the bath and an elegantly attired woman on skis.

70. See Albert Sauvy, *Histoire économique de la France entre les deux guerres*, vol. 2 (Paris: Editions Economica, 1984), pp. 35-37; Evelyne Sullerot, "Condition de la femme," in Albert Sauvy, *Histoire économique de la France entre les deux guerres*, vol. 3 (Paris: Editions Economica, 1984), pp. 195-209; and Jean-Louis Robert, "Women and Work in France during the First World War," in Richard Wall and Jay Winter, eds., *The Upheaval of War: Family, Work and Welfare in Europe, 1914-1918* (Cambridge: Cambridge University Press, 1989), pp. 251-66. Note especially the tables provided by Robert (p. 262), which show that women's participation in the paid labor force reached its apogee in World War I and then declined in a linear fashion for the next fifty years. Sullerot's figures (p. 199) are slightly different for the post-1921 period, but indicate the same trend. Both authors also demonstrate the restructuring of female labor in the interwar years

toward greater participation in the modern sectors of the economy.

71. See Reynolds, "Women, Men and the 1936 Strikes in France," but given the broad-based nature of the strikes, they are best understood as a combined community and workplace insurgency. Reynolds' search for evidence of women's activism is therefore somewhat misplaced by her exclusive concentration on the workplace.

72. Cited in Schneider, "The Eugenics Movement in France," pp. 100-01.

73. Schneider, "The Eugenics Movement in France," pp. 100-02.

74. Delpla, "Les Communistes français et la sexualité," p. 142.

75. None of this seems to have had much impact on the PCF's membership, which remained overwhelmingly male. In 1926, women composed only 1.72 percent of the membership, in 1946, by the PCF's own reckoning, only 11.2 percent. See Annie Kriegel, *Les Communistes français dans leur premier demi siècle 1920-1970*, 2nd ed. (Paris: Editions du Seuil, 1985), pp. 76-85, figures pp. 76-78. It may be, however, that where the PCF controlled local politics, its support among women far surpassed the national profile of the party. By 1966 the proportion had risen to 25.5 percent, though Kriegel points out that the postwar increase does not indicate greater success on the part of the party, but greater fidelity of women to the PCF, since the proportion increased as the overall membership of the party declined. Significantly, figures for the postwar period indicate that of the female membership, almost half were not involved in the paid labor force, underscoring once again the futility of appealing to women only as workers. Postwar voting statistics indicate that throughout the Fourth and Fifth Republics, the PCF electorate has been the most masculine of any major party. It is hard to imagine that had there existed female suffrage before 1944, the PCF would have done any better among women than in the 1947 national elections, when the party's electorate was 62 percent male and 38 percent female. (Kriegel, *Les Communistes français*, p. 84).

76. This and subsequent points follow François Caron, *Histoire économique de la France XIXe-XXe siècles* (Paris: Armand Colin, 1981), pp. 158-59, 166-67, 190-93, 196-201. A more sanguine interpretation of the performance of the economy in the interwar years is provided by Richard F. Kuisel, *Capitalism and the State in Modern France: Renovation and Economic Management in the Twentieth Century* (Cambridge: Cambridge University Press, 1981). Caron's synthesis, as well as those presented in Fernand Braudel and Ernest Labrousse, eds., *Histoire économique et sociale de la France* 4:2 (Paris: Presses Universitaires de France, 1980), have the virtues of abandoning the terminology of backwardness, and locating the particular features of French economic development within major structural conditions.

77. The economic crisis came later to France and its impact was far more limited than in other industrialized countries. See Caron, *Histoire économique*, pp. 200-04 and Claude Fohlen, "France 1920-1970," in Carlo M. Cipolla, ed. *The Fontana Economic History of Europe*, vol. 6:

Contemporary Economies, part 1 (Sussex: Harvester Press, 1979), pp. 86-91. Foreign workers bore the initial brunt of firings, and many firms chose to reduce the workday rather than institute layoffs. In 1935 the unemployment rate in France was 14.5 percent: Walter Galenson, "The Labour Force and Labour Problems in Europe 1920-1970," in Cipolla, *Fontana Economic History* 5:1, p. 143. Touchard and Bodin argue that the direct impact of the Depression was probably greater on the middle classes than on the industrial proletariat. ("L'État du opinion au début de l'année 1936," in *Léon Blum*, p. 53.)

78. See for example Bertrand Badie, "Les Grèves du Front populaire aux usines Renault," *Mouvement social* 81 (1972): 73-75; Jean-Paul Depretto and Sylvie V. Schweitzer, *Le Communisme à l'Usine* (Roubaix: Edires, 1984), pp. 20-43; and Patrick Fridenson, "Automobile Workers in France and Their Work, 1914-83," in Steven L. Kaplan and Cynthia J. Koepp, eds., *Work in France: Representations, Meaning, Organization, and Practice* (Ithaca: Cornell University Press, 1986), pp. 514-30. On the related aircraft industry, see Herrick Chapman, *State Capitalism and Working-Class Radicalism in the French Aircraft Industry* (Berkeley and Los Angeles: University of California Press, 1991), esp. pp. 43-54, 89-94.

79. On the mines, Odette Hardy-Hémery, "Rationalisation technique et rationalisation du travail à la Compagnie des Mines d'Anzin," *Mouvement social* 72 (1970): 3-48; Raymond Hainsworth, "Les Grèves du Front populaire de mai et juin 1936: Une nouvelle analyse fondée sur l'étude de ces grèves dans le bassin houiller du Nord et du Pas-de-Calais," *Mouvement social* 96 (1976): 5-7; Aimée Moutet, "La Rationalisation dans les mines du Nord à l'épreuve du Front populaire: Etude d'après les sources imprimées," *Mouvement social* 135 (April-June 1986): 63-99. Other rationalization measures included the mechanization of transport, which entailed constructing long belts as well as railways and passages large enough to encompass diesel engines. The intensified pace of work and the noise of machinery, which prevented skilled miners from listening to the cracks and crevices for danger signs, led also to higher accident rates. See the accident statistics in Hardy-Hénery, "Rationalisation technique," p. 33.

80. As Julian Jackson argues in his fine summary of conditions in the workplace and working-class attitudes. See *The Popular Front*, pp. 85-112.

81. See Badie, "Les Grèves du Front populaire;" Hainsworth, "Les Grèves du Front populaire du mai et juin 1936;" Chapman, *State Capitalism and Working-Class Radicalism*, pp. 75-100; and Depretto and Schweitzer, *Le Communisme à l'Usine*, pp. 181-202, all of whom convincingly argue that the strikes cannot be seen as simply spontaneous outbursts and that PCF and ex-CGTU militants played critical roles in organizing the movements. Jackson, *The Popular Front*, pp. 85-104, summarizes the events and the historiographical debate.

82. Hardy-Hémery, "Rationalisation technique," p. 37.

83. Adrian Rossiter, "Popular Front Economic Policy and the Matignon Negotiations," *Historical Journal* 30:3 (September 1987): 663-84.

84. George Ross, *Workers and Communists in France: From Popular Front to Eurocommunism* (Berkeley and Los Angeles: University of California Press, 1982), pp. 9-10 and Kriegel, *Les Communistes français*, pp. 90, 96. For a very good case study of communist implantation in the workplace, which accords major importance to the combination of workplace militancy and state interventionism, see Chapman, *State Capitalism and Working-Class Radicalism*.

85. Kriegel, *Les Communistes français*, p. 98.

86. The rise in CGT membership was greatest where the communist-led federation, the CGTU, had been strongest, and, in general, among the quintessential twentieth-century proletarian, the semi-skilled mass-production worker, who had been largely ignored by the CGT in the preceding years. See Jean Bruhat, "La CGT," in Réné Rémond and Janine Bourdin, eds., *La France et les Français en 1938-1939* (Paris: Presses de la Fondation Nationale des Science Politiques, 1978), pp. 160-62, 168-69 and Ross, *Workers and Communists in France*, pp. 7-10.

87. See for example Chambaz, "L'implantation du Parti communiste français à Ivry" and Jacques Girault, "L'implantation du Parti communiste français dans la region parisienne," in Girault, ed., *L'implantation du Parti communiste français*, pp. 61-117 and 147-77; Jackson, *Popular Front*, p. 92; Badie, "Les Gréves du Front populaire," p. 91.

88. Hardy-Hémery, "Rationalisation technique," pp. 36-41; Moutet, "La rationalisation das les mines du Nord," pp. 85-97.

89. Adrian Rossiter, "The Blum government, the Conseil National Économique and Economic Policy," in Alexander and Graham, *The French and Spanish Popular Fronts*, pp. 156-70; Jean-Pierre Rioux, "La conciliation et l'arbitrage obligatoire des conflits du travail," in Réné Rémond and Janine Bourdin, *Edouard Daladier, Chef du Gouvernement* (Paris: Presses de la Fondation Nationale des Sciences Politiques, 1977), pp. 112-28; Antoine Prost, "Le Climat social," in *Edouard Daladier*, pp. 99-111. For a good summary of the social measures of the Popular Front, including collective bargaining, see Étienne Gout, Pierre Juvigny, Michel Mousel, "La Politique sociale du Front populaire," in *Léon Blum*, pp. 241-76. Despite misgivings among some workers and worker representatives, the CGT, SFIO, and PCF all continued to support compulsory arbitration, and limited their attacks to the manner of its implementation by the Daladier government.

90. Prost, "Le Climat social," p. 110.

91. As is sometimes the tenor of interpretions that emphasize the joyous, festive nature of the Popular Front, such as Touchard and Bodin, "L'état d'opinion," pp. 55-61 and Prost, "Les Grèves de Juin 1936," pp. 81-83. Philippe Burrin, in a very interesting article, "Poings levées et bras tendus: La contagion des symboles au temps du Front populaire," *Vingtième siècle* 11 (July-September 1986): 5-20, sees the symbolism of the Popular Front as a substitute for revolution. This may well be the case, but Burrin writes as if nothing concrete was accomplished in this period.

92. See Rossiter, "The Blum Government, the Conseil National Économique and Economic Policy" and Chapman, *State Capitalism and Working-Class Radicalism*.

93. As is probably clear, my position here differs diametrically from that of the doyenne of PCF studies, Annie Kriegel, whose most renowned contention is that the PCF has formed a counter-society, of but not in French society. See especially *Les Communistes français*.

Three problems arise with Kriegel's interpretation. First, the notion of society, in and of itself, permits of no "exteriority." By definition, individuals and institutions that are born and develop within a society are influenced by it; they are a part of that society and *cannot* exist outside of it. In the stark terms in which Kriegel sometimes couches her coinage of a counter-society, the concept remains nothing more than an abstraction. Second, the success of the PCF in forging a mass base has demonstrated precisely the opposite of a counter-society. At least some of the institutions of French society have been, as argued above, exceedingly porous, enabling the PCF to become very much a part of French society at the same time that it has presented an ideological alternative to it. Third, the argument about whether or not the PCF has become reformist is vacuous if only discussed in terms of ideology and programs. What is clear is that since the 1930s (with the exception of the war years) the PCF has occupied positions of political power within the institutions of French society. Its *functional role* has been reformist, even while its ideology has, at least until very recently, been revolutionary.

Ultimately, Kriegel's reasoning becomes tautalogical: The PCF exists outside of French society; to the extent that it has pierced the barriers and has entered within the charmed circle of that society, it is only to preserve its "outsider" character—it becomes a part of France to maintain its exteriority. (*Les Communistes français*, p. 358.)

Georges Lavau's definition of the PCF as having a "tributary function," i.e., defending the interests of workers and other subordinate groups, but within the confines of the existing structures, is ultimately far more convincing than Kriegel's formulations. See Lavau, "Le Parti communiste dans le système politique français," in *Le Communisme en France*, Cahiers de la Fondation Nationale des Sciences Politiques no. 175 (Paris: Armand Colin, 1969), pp. 7-65. Among other commentators on the PCF, Isaac Aviv, "Le PCF dans le système français des années 1930 à la fin de la IVe République," *Mouvement social* 104 (1978): 75-93, analyzes how the ideology and values—the "myths," in his terminology—of the PCF have served to integrate the party and the working class into the nation, yet utterly neglects to examine in tandem with ideology the functional role of the party. Daniel Brower, *The New Jacobins: The French Communist Party and the Popular Front* (Ithaca: Cornell University Press, 1968) emphasizes the party's fusion of proletarian revolution and Jacobin republicanism, but without analyzing the tension inherent in this construction.

94. See also Tony Judt, "Une historiographie pas comme les autres: The French Communists and their History," *European Studies Review* 12:4 (October 1982): 445-78.

95. It is misplaced, therefore, to search for some metahistorical character to the PCF. Annie Kriegel's unyielding contention that the character of the PCF is to be found by analyzing its essential Bolshevism is one variant of this approach. Among her many works, see especially "Les communistes français et la question du pouvoir (1920-1939)," *Annales: économies, sociétés, civilisations* 21:6 (November-December 1966): 1245-58; "Léon Blum et le Parti communiste," in Renouvin and Rémond, *Léon Blum*, pp. 125-35; and *Les Communistes française*. In the PCF metahistorical version, at least until the 1980s, the history of the party constitutes a seamless web. There were no ruptures, merely "adaptations" or "corrections" as the party moved along... to what is not always clear. Or there is a third alternative: the PCF continually betraying the interests of the working class. A recent version can be found in Helen Graham and Paul Preston, "The Popular Front and the Struggle against Fascism," in Graham and Preston, eds., *The Popular Front in Europe* (New York: St. Martin's Press, 1987), pp. 1-19. Tony Judt makes the point about the inconsistencies of the PCF and is highly critical of the its metahistorical version ("Une historiographie pas comme les autres," p. 461). But his fulsome praise of Kriegel blinds him to her variant of this approach.

96. There is a very substantial literature on the wartime strikes. See, among others, Paolo Spriano, *Storia del Partito comunista italiano*, vol. 5: *La Resistenza. Togliatti e il partito nuovo* (Turin: Einaudi, 1975), pp. 20-37, 217-81, 338-61; Sergio Turone, *Storia del sindacato in Italia (1943-1969): Dalla Resistenza all' "autunno caldo"* (Rome: Laterza, 1975), pp. 14-29, 33-40, 62-72, 77-84; Claudio Dellavalle, "La classe operaia piedmontese nella guerra di Liberazione," in Aldo Agosti and Gian Mario Bravo, eds., *Storia del movimento operaio del socialismo e delle lotte sociali in Piemonte* (Bari: De Donato, 1980), pp. 328-58; and, most recently, the very careful reconstruction and (typically) original analysis of Tim Mason, "Gli scioperi di Torino del marzo 1943," in Francesca Ferratini Tosi, et. al., eds., *L'Italia nella seconda guerra mondiale e nella Resistenza* (Milan: Franco Angeli Libri, 1988), pp. 399-422.

97. B. Salvati, "The Rebirth of Italian Trade Unionism, 1943-54," in S.J. Woolf, ed., *The Rebirth of Italy, 1943-50* (London: Longman, 1972), p. 189.

98. In the last five months of 1942, an average of 3.6 strikes per month occurred in the northern region of Piedmont, Lombardy, and Emilia; in January and February an average of fourteen over a still larger region. Umberto Massola, "Gli scioperi del '43," in Ernesto Ragionieri, ed., *I comunisti a Torino 1919-1972: Lezioni e testimonianze* (Rome: Riuniti, 1974), pp. 137-38.

99. On the reestablishment of the internal commissions see Spriano, *Storia del Partito comunista italiano*, vol. 5, pp. 13-14; Turone, *Storia del sindacato in Italia*, pp. 33-38.

100. Umberto Massola had been charged with this task by the party leadership, and secretly returned to the country in 1941. By the summer of 1942, he had managed to start printing clandestinely *l'Unità*, which began to appear with some frequency in the factories. See Aldo Agosti, "Relazione," in *I comunisti a Torino*, p. 103.

101. Turone, *Storia del sindacato in Italia*, pp. 70-71, 82-83.

102. Turone, *Storia del sindacato in Italia*, pp. 101-02.

103. The debate on fascist economic policy remains vibrant. In general, see Gianni Toniolo, *L'economia dell'italia fascista* (Rome: Editori Laterza, 1980), who perhaps goes too far in denying any unitary character to the period, and Gualberto Gualerni, *Industria e fascismo: Per una interpretazione dello sviluppo economico italiano tra le due guerre* (Milan: Vita e Pensiero, 1976), who stresses the progression of capitalism. Rosario Romeo, *Breve storia de la grande industria in italia 1861-1961* (1961; Bologna: Cappelli Editore, 1980), is especially skeptical about an economic advance in the fascist period, while Charles S. Maier, "The Economics of Fascism and Nazism," in his *In Search of Stability: Explorations in Historical Political Economy* (Cambridge: Cambridge University Press, 1987), takes a rather diffident approach. Maier argues that the economy under fascism expanded, but at very moderate rate and with limited structural transformations. (pp. 91-96) But which economy performed well in the interwar period? Gualerni's emphasis on the progression of of capitalism is supported by some telling statistical evidence: In the conditions of relative stagnation in the interwar years, average annual growth rates of 2.2 percent, and 3.6 percent for industrial production, were highly respectable, even if these rates stood below the great years of advance prior to 1914 and after 1945. The crucial industries of the "second industrial revolution"—chemical, electric power generation, as well as engineering—expanded at even higher rates, and generally survived cyclical downswings in better shape. See Toniolo, *L'economia dell'italia fascista*, pp. 9, 68-70, 128-31, 165-74, 322-29. The overall decline in production between 1929 and 1933 lay close to the European average, and was only greater than Norway, Denmark, Switzerland, and the U.K. Unemployment rose from 300,000 to over one million in 1932, but even these rates were not particularly high in comparison with other European countries. See Salvatore LaFrancesca, *La politica economia del fascismo*, (1972; Rome: Laterza, 1976), p. 48. For comparisons see the table in B.R. Mitchell, "Statistical Appendix," in Carlo M. Cipolla, ed., *The Fontana Economic History of Europe* 6:2 (Sussex: Harvester Press, 1979), p. 667: in 1937, the Italian rate was already down to 4.6 percent.

104. See Dellavalle, "La classe operaia piemontese nella guerra di Liberazione," pp. 308-28. Dellavalle notes that the process of industrial expansion in the metal-working and engineering industries of the Piedmont

included medium-sized firms as well as the giant FIAT works.

105. Agosti, "Relazione," p. 105.

106. This comes across in Victoria de Grazia's important study, *The Culture of Consent: Mass Organization of Leisure in Fascist Italy* (Cambridge: Cambridge University Press, 1981), especially pp. 60-93. On the formation of the fascist system I have relied especially on Adrian Lyttelton, *The Seizure of Power: Fascism in Italy, 1919-1929* (London: Weidenfeld and Nicolson, 1973).

107. Martin Clark, *Modern Italy, 1871-1982* (London: Longman, 1984), pp. 248-49.

108. Turone, *Storia del sindacato in Italia*, pp. 62-63, 73-77.

109. Dellavalle, "La classe operaia piemontese nella guerra di Liberazione," p. 340; Liliana Lanzardo, "I Consigli di gestione nella strategia della collaborazione," in Aris Accornero, ed., *Problemi del movimento sindacale in Italia 1943-1973*, Fondazione Giangiacomo Feltrinelli, *Annali* 16 (1974-1975), pp. 325-26.

110. Especially for the PCI's approach to women in its early years, see Nadia Spano and Fiamma Camarlinghi, *La questione femminile nella politica del PCI 1921-1963* (Rome: Ed. Donne e Politica, 1972). The quote is from an article by Camilla Ravera, "Il nostro femminismo," cited in *ibid.*, pp. 27-29: "...nella capacità femminile creare e rendere dolce e riposante l'intimità, la casa, la famiglia."

111. Cited in Spano, *La questione femminile*, p. 39.

112. Dellavalle, "La classe operaia piemontese nella guerra di Liberazione," p. 317.

113. On population policy Clark, *Modern Italy*, pp. 274-76. "Hysteria" is his apt phrase. (p. 275) In general on fascist policy towards women, see Victoria De Grazia, *How Fascism Ruled Women: Italy, 1922-1945* (Berkeley and Los Angeles: University of California Press, 1992).

114. Cited in Clark, *Modern Italy*, p. 276.

115. Clark, *Modern Italy*, p. 276.

116. For some indications of the forms of women's activism, see Giuletta Ascoli, "L'Udi tra emancipazione e libèrazione (1943-1964)," *Problemi del socialismo* 17:4 (October/December 1976): 111-13; Alba Mora, "Per una storia dell'associazionismo femminile a Parma: GDD e UDI tra emancipazione e tradizione (1943-1946)," in Fiorenzo Sicuri, ed., *Comunisti a Parma: Atti del convegno tenutosi a Parma il 7 Novembre 1981* (Parma: STEP Cooperativa, 1986), pp. 299-307; De Grazia, *How Fascism Ruled Women*, pp. 272-88; Lucia Chiavola Birnbaum, *Liberazione della donna: Feminism in Italy* (Middletown, CT: Wesleyan University Press, 1986), pp. 41-50; Spano and Camarlinghi, *La questione femminile*, pp. 87-95; Miriam Mafai, *L'apprendistato della politica: Le donne italiane nel dopoguerra* (Rome: Riuniti, 1979), pp. 68-92; and Ada Marchesini Gobetti, "Perchè erano tante nella Resistenza," *Rinascita* 3 (March 1961): 245-51.

117. Ascoli, "L'Udi tra emancipazione e libèrazione," p. 112.

118. At the end of the war, women composed 15.6 of the party membership. By 1948, the figure had risen to 22.1 percent, and by 1950 to 25.3 percent. Celso Ghini, "Gli iscritti al partito e alla FGCI 1943/1979," in Massimo Illardi and Aris Accornero, eds. *Il Partito comunista italiano: Struttura e storia dell'organizzazione 1921/1979*, Fondazione Giangiacomo Feltrinelli, *Annali* 21 (1981), p. 269. These figures were considerably higher than those for the PCF and KPD. From 1950 down to 1980, the PCI's proportion of women members remained about one-quarter.

119. Fausto Anderlini, "La cellula," in Ilardi and Accorrnero, *Il Partito comunista italiano*, pp. 207-10 and Giordano Sivini, "Le Parti communiste: Struture et fonctionnement," in *Sociologie du communisme en Italie*, Cahiers de la Fondation Nationale des Sciences Politiques no. 194 (Paris: Armand Colin, 1974), p. 88. At the highpoint in the mid-1950s, there were about 14,000 female cells; by 1960, the number had declined to 8000-9000 and by 1967 to 2,100, and these predominantly in the red regions.

120. See especially Ascoli, "L'Udi tra emancipazione e libèrazione," quote p. 117. For an introduction to the UDI in English, Judith Adler Hellman, *Journeys among Women: Feminism in Five Italian Cities* (New York: Oxford University Press, 1987), pp. 27-54 and Birnbaum, *Liberazione della donna*, pp. 51-64.

121. Cited in Ascoli, "L'Udi tra emancipazione e libèrazione," p. 114.

122. Ascoli, "L'Udi tra emancipazione e libèrazione," pp. 116-19.

123. See especially Togliatti's speeches to the First Women's Conference of the PCI in June 1945 and to the UDI in September 1946, published in Palmiro Togliatti, *L'emancipazione femminile* (Rome: Editori Riuniti, 1965), pp. 21-71.

124. Cited in Turone, *Storia del sindacato in Italia*, pp. 98-99.

125. D.J. Travis, "Communism in Modena: The Provincial Origins of the Partito comunista italiano (1943-1945)," *Historical Journal* 29:4 (December 1986): 884.

126. See especially Paul Ginsborg, "The Communist Party and the Agrarian Question in Southern Italy, 1943-48," *History Workshop* 17 (Spring 1984): 81-101.

127. See Ginsborg, "The Communist Party and the Agrarian Question," for a clear summary and evaluation.

128. For some relevant statistical information, see Sivini, "Le parti communiste: Structure et fonctionnement," p. 89; Sidney Tarrow, "Le Parti communiste e la société italienne," in *Sociologie du communisme in Italie*, pp. 22-27; and Ghini, "Gli iscritti al partito e all FGCI."

129. Discussions of the *partito nouvo* abound. Among others see Spriano, *Storia del Partito comunista italiano*, vol. 5; Donald Sassoon, *The Strategy of the Italian Communist Party: From the Resistance to the Historic Compromise* (New York: St. Martin's Press, 1981), pp. 8-58; Alessandro Natta, "La Resistenza e la formazione del 'partito nuovo,'" in Paolo Spriano,

et. al., *Problemi di storia del Partito comunista italiano* (Rome: Editori Riuniti, 1971), pp. 57-83; Ernesto Ragionieri, "Il PCI nella Resistenza: La nascita del 'partito nuovo,'" *Studi Storici* 10:1 (January-March 1969): 83-113. For an insightful synthesis in English, Paul Ginsborg, *A History of Contemporary Italy: Society and Politics 1943-1988* (London: Penguin Books, 1990), pp. 42-48, 79-88. Natta and Ragionieri provide the most interesting historical discussion of the two terms that Togliatti coined to describe the PCI's strategy. Togliatti himself said that he adapted the *il partito nuovo* from Lenin's "party of a new type," but one might also point out the linkage with Togliatti's important article from the Spanish Civil War, in which he described the Spanish Republic as a "democracy of a new type." See Palmiro Togliatti, *Opere*, vol. 4, part 1, ed. Franco Andreucci and Paolo Spriano (Rome: Riuniti, 1979), pp. 139-54.

130. It is curious that a number of excellent studies on Italy and on the PCI neglect Togliatti's political involvement in the 1920s as a source of explanation for his policies in the 1940s. See, for example, Sassoon, *The Strategy of the Italian Communist Party* and Ginsborg, *Contemporary Italy*. In contrast, Ernesto Ragionieri stressed in all of his writings the essential continuities in Togliatti's political ideas from the 1920s to *il partito nuovo*. See, for example, "Il PCI nella Resistenza: La nascita del 'partito nuovo,'" pp. 84-91 and "Il giudizio sul fascismo. La lotta contro il fascismo. I rapporti con l'Internazionale comunista," in *Problemi di storia del Partito comunista italiano*, pp. 33-55.

131. This is often the case both with PCI commentators, e.g. Alessandro Natta, "La Resitenza e la formazione del 'partito nuovo,'" and those critical of the party, e.g. Federico Mancini, "The Theoretical Roots of Italian Communism: Worker Democracy and Political Party in Gramsci's Thinking," and Lawrence Gray, "From Gramsci to Togliatti: The *Partito Nuovo* and the Mass Basis of Italian Communism," in Simon Serfaty and Lawrence Gray, eds., *The Italian Communist Party: Yesterday, Today, and Tomorrow* (Westport: Greenwood Press, 1980), pp. 3-36. But it also makes little sense to dismiss any connection between the mass party of the Resistance and postwar years and the Gramscian legacy, a trait typical of the writings of Tony Judt. See, for example, "'The Spreading Notion of the Town,'" and also Travis, "Communism in Modena," which is an important article that places the emergence of the PCI within its local context, but goes too far by concluding: "...communism on the ground created its own set of political ideas and wrote a new definition of political allegiance during the Resistance." (p.895) This grants excessive *ideological* autonomy to the local PCI, and inaccurately dismisses the historical and ideological legacy of the party.

132. Or, in Gramsci's renowned formulation, "In Russia the State was everything, civil society was primordial and gelatinous; in the West there was a proper relationship between State and civil society; and when the State trembled, a sturdy structure of civil society was at once revealed." (*Selections from the Prison Notebooks*, ed. Quintin Hoare and Geoffrey Nowell Smith (New York: International Publishers, 1971), p. 238.)

133. Perhaps less significant for the overall history of Italy than for the party itself, many party militants found the Yugoslav example of a communist party fighting its way to the exclusive hold on political power far more compelling than Togliatti's *partito nuovo*. This was especially the case among members whose formative experiences were not those of the Resistance but of the conspiratorial underground and party work in a communist movement deeply influenced by Stalinism. See Yedid Jodice, "L'organizzazione del 'partito nuovo': Il PCI torinese nel 1945-56," in *Storia del movimento operaio del socialismo e delle loite sociali in Piemonte*, pp. 71-121; Ragionieri, "Il PCI nella Resitanza: La nascita del 'partito nuovo;'" and, generally, Spriano, *Storia del Partito comunista italiano*, vol. 5.

Here I would disagree with Sidney Tarrow's distinction between the strategies of the social democratic parties and the PCI, which he develops in "Le parti communiste e la société italienne," pp. 3, 15-17. While the classic Kautskyist strategy indeed involved the construction of autonomous party bastions "outside" of the existing structures, the rationale for government involvement of the SPD in the Weimar Republic and the SPÖ in the Austrian First Republic was little different than that of the PCI after 1944: to work within existing institutions to transform them. Of course, this also presumed the willingness of the respective elites to tolerate a social democratic presence, a highly dubious presumption.

134. See Lanzardo, "Il Consigli di gestione" and for the example of Fiat, Renzo Gianotti, *Lotte e organizzazioni di classe alla FIAT (1948-1970)* (Bari: De Donato, 1970), pp. 29-41.

135. Ascoli, "L'Udi tra emancipazione e libèrazione," p. 128.

136. Compare, for example, *l'Unità* 12 may 1945 and the electoral propaganda published on 10 April 1948 and 18 April 1948.

137. Ascoli, L'Udi tra emanzipazione e libèrazione." For examples of women's activism in the Piedmont, Aurelia Camparini, "Lotte e organizzazione delle donne dalla Liberazione agli anni Sessante," in Agosti and Bravo, eds., *Stori del movimento operaio del socialism e delle lotte sociali in Piemonte*, vol. 4, pp. 555-99. Contrast *l'Unità* 8 March 1946 and 8 March 1948 on the varied treatment of International Women's Day in the party press.

138. On the party and agrarian issues see Sidney Tarrow, *Peasant Communism in Southern Italy* (New Haven: Yale University Press, 1967); Giorgio Amendola, "Il PCI all'opposizione. La lotta contro lo scelbismo," in *Problemi di storia del Partito comunista italiano*, pp. 105-29; and Ginsborg, "The Communist Party and the Agrarian Question." Amendola characterizes the land seizures as the "continuation of the Resistance on the southern terrain." (p. 121.)

139. See Tarrow, "Le parti communiste et la société italienne," pp. 37-53, for a longterm analysis of this phenomenon.

140. See Charles Tilly, "Warmaking as Statemaking," in Peter B. Evans, Dietrich Rueschemeyer, and Theda Skocpol, eds., *Bringing the State Back In* (Cambridge: Cambridge University Press, 1985), pp. 169-91.

141. See the major statements in Evans, Rueschemeyer, and Skocpol, *Bringing the State Back In* and Charles Bright and Susan Harding, eds., *Statemaking and Social Movements: Essays in History and Theory* (Ann Arbor: University of Michigan Press, 1984). For the neo-Marxist debate, Nicos Poulantzas, *Political Power and Social Classes* (London: NLB & S&W, 1973) and Ralph Miliband, *The State in Capitalist Society* (New York: Basic Books, 1969), among others.

Geograpers and other social scientists strongly influenced by geography have provided the major corrective to the neglect of the locality and the local state. For some examples, which offer differing perspectives on the local state, see Andrew Kirby, "State, Local State, Context, and Spatiality: A Reappraisal of State Theory," in James A. Caporaso, ed., *The Elusive State: International and Comparative Perspectives* (London: Sage, 1989), pp. 204-26; Manuel Castells, *The City and the Grassroots* (Berkeley and Los Angeles: University of California Press, 1983); Michael Dear, "A Theory of the Local State," in Alan D. Burnett and Peter J. Taylor, eds., *Political Studies from Spatial Perspectives* (Chichester: Wiley, 1981), pp. 183-200; Agnew, *Place and Politics*; and Harvey, *Consciousness and the Urban Experience*.

142. As in J.P. Nettl's classic essay, "The State as a Conceptual Variable," *World Politics* 20:4 (July 1968): 559-92.

143. My argument in favor of some lines of continuity between old and new oppositional movements is influenced by David Harvey's contention that postmodernism is not so much a break with as a reshaping of modernism. See Harvey, *The Condition of Postmodernity: An Enquiry into the Origins of Cultural Change* (Oxford: Basil Blackwell, 1989). The literature on new social movements is vast. For some arguments in favor of "newness," see Claus Offe, "Challenging the Boundaries of Institutional Politics: Social Movements since the 1960s," in Charles S. Maier, *Changing Boundaries of the Political: Essays on the Evolving Balance between the State and Society, Public and Private in Europe* (Cambridge: Cambridge University Press, 1987), pp. 63-105 (among many other works by Offe); Ernesto Laclau, *New Reflections on the Revolution of Our Time* (London: Verso, 1990); and Ernesto Laclau and Chantal Mouffe, *Hegemony and Socialist Strategy: Towards a Radical Democratic Politics* (London: Verso, 1985). For a sharp critique and counter-argument, Tarrow, *Struggle, Politics, and Reform*, esp. pp. 57-69.

144. Note also Geoff Eley, "International Communism in the Heyday of Stalin," *New Left Review* 157 (May/June 1986): 98, in discussing the period of the Resistance and the immediate post war years, comments: "One of the most striking things in this situation was how far the new departures were generated from the empirical experiences of the parties concerned, and how little they owed to the directive strategy of an international communist centre."

145. Tarrow, "Le Parti communiste et la société italienne," p. 22.

146. Notably, Donald L. M. Blackmer and Sidney Tarrow, eds., *Communism in Italy and France* (Princeton: Princeton University Press, 1975); Peter Lange, George Ross, and Maurizio Vannicelli, *Unions, Change and Crisis: French and Italian Union Strategy and the Political Economy, 1945-1980* (London: George Allen & Unwin, 1982); and the two volumes, though published separately, that grew out of a 1968 colloquium at the Fondation Nationale des Sciences Politiques: *Le communisme en France* and *Sociologie du communisme en italie.*

147. As was especially current in the heyday of Eurocommunism. See, for example, Carl Boggs and David Plotke, eds., *The Politics of Eurocommunism: Socialism in Transition* (Boston: South End Press, 1980).

148. As Ross, *Workers and Communists in France*, never tires of pointing out: "The new industrial working class in France faced a unique form of bourgeois society." (p. 1) "The uniqueness of twentieth-century French labor history begins with World War I." (p. 3)

149. See the critique of this approach by David Blackbourn and Geoff Eley, *The Peculiarities of German History: Bourgeois Society and Politics in Nineteenth-Century Germany* (Oxford: Oxford University Press, 1984).

Bibliography

Accornero, Aris, ed. *Problemi del movimento sindacale in Italia 1943-1973*, Fondazione Giangiacomo Feltrinelli, *Annali* 16 (1974-1975).

Agnew, John A. *Place and Politics: The Geographical Mediation of State and Society* (Boston: Allen & Unwin, 1987).

Agosti, Aldo. "Relazione," in Ernesto Ragionieri, ed. *I comunisti a Torino 1919-1972: Lezioni e testimonianze* (Rome: Riuniti, 1974), pp. 101-33.

Agosti, Aldo and Bravo, Gian Mario, eds. *Storia del movimento operaio del socialismo e delle lotte sociali in Piemonte*, vol. 4 (Bari: De Donato, 1980).

Amendola, Giorgio. "Il PCI all'opposizione. La lotta contro lo scelbismo," in Paolo Spriano, et. al., *Problemi di storia del Partito comunista italiano* (Rome: Editori Riuniti, 1971), pp. 105-29.

Anderlini, Fausto. "La cellula," in Massimo Illardi and Aris Accornero, eds. *Il Partito comunista italiano: Struttura e storia dell'organizzazione 1921/1979*, Fondazione Giangiacomo Feltrinelli, *Annali* 21 (1981): 185-226.

Arbeiter-Illustrierte-Zeitung, Berlin (1926 to 1932).

Arendt, Hans-Jürgen. "Weibliche Mitglieder der KPD in der Weimarer Republik: Zahlenmäßige Stärke und soziale Stellung," *Beiträge zur Geschichte der Arbeiterbewegung* 19 (1977): 652-60.

Ascoli, Giulietta. "L'Udi tra emancipazione e libèrazione (1943-1964)," *Problemi del socialismo* 17:4 (October/December 1976): 109-59.

Aviv, Isaac. "Le PCF dans le système français des années 1930 à la fin de la IVe République," *Mouvement social* 104 (1978): 75-93.

Badie, Bertrand. "Les Grèves du Front populaire aux usines Renault," *Mouvement social* 81 (1972): 69-109.

Bahne, Siegfried. "Die Erwerbslosenpolitik der KPD in der Weimarer Republik," in Hans Mommsen and Winfried Schulze, eds. *Vom Elend der Handarbeit: Probleme historischer Unterschichtenforschung* (Stuttgart: Klett-Cotta, 1981), pp. 477-96.

Barbé, Henri. "Souvenirs de militant et de dirigeant communiste," (typescript, Hoover Institution Archives).

Bauer, Karin. *Clara Zetkin und die proletarische Frauenbewegung* (Berlin: Oberbaum Verlag, 1978).

Bessel, Richard. "'Eine nicht allzu große Beunruhigung des

Arbeitsmarktes': Frauenarbeit und Demobilmachung in Deutschland nach dem Ersten Weltkrieg," *Geschichte und Gesellschaft* 9:2 (1983): 211-29.

Birnbaum, Lucia Chiavola. *Liberazione della donna: Feminism in Italy* (Middletown, CT: Wesleyan University Press, 1986).

Blackbourn, David and Eley, Geoff. *The Peculiarities of German History: Bourgeois Society and Politics in Nineteenth-Century Germany* (Oxford: Oxford University Press, 1984).

Blackmer, Donald L. M. and Tarrow, Sidney, eds. *Communism in Italy and France* (Princeton: Princeton University Press, 1975).

Boggs, Carl and Plotke, David, eds. *The Politics of Eurocommunism: Socialism in Transition* (Boston: South End Press, 1980).

Borkenau, Franz. *World Communism: A History of the Communist International* (New York: Norton, 1939).

Braudel, Fernand and Labrousse, Ernest, eds. *Histoire économique et sociale de la France* 4:2 (Paris: Presses Universitaires de France, 1980).

Braunthal, Julius. *History of the International*, vol. 2: *1914-1943* (New York: Praeger, 1967).

Bremme, Gabriele. *Die politische Rolle der Frau in Deutschland: Eine Untersuchung über den Einfluß der Frauen bei Wahlen und ihre Teilnahme in Partei und Parlament* (Göttingen: Vandenhoeck & Ruprecht, 1956).

Bridenthal, Renate; Grossmann, Atina; and Kaplan, Marion, eds. *When Biology Became Destiny: Women in Weimar and Nazi Germany* (New York: Monthly Review Press, 1984).

Bridenthal, Renate and Koonz, Claudia. "Beyond *Kinder, Küche, Kirche*: Weimar Women in Politics and Work," in Renate Bridenthal, Atina Grossmann, and Marion Kaplan, eds. *When Biology Became Destiny: Women in Weimar and Nazi Germany* (New York: Monthly Review Press, 1984), pp. 33-65.

Bright, Charles and Harding, Susan, eds. *Statemaking and Social Movements: Essays in History and Theory* (Ann Arbor: University of Michigan Press, 1984).

Brower, Daniel. *The New Jacobins: The French Communist Party and the Popular Front* (Ithaca: Cornell University Press, 1968).

Bruhat, Jean. "La CGT," in Réné Rémond and Janine Bourdin, eds. *La France et les Français en 1938-1939* (Paris: Presses de la Fondation Nationale des Science Politiques, 1978).

Burrin, Philippe. "Diplomatie soviétique, Internationale communiste et PCF au tournant du Front populaire (1934-35)," *Relations internationales* 45 (Spring 1986): 19-34.

_____. "Poings levées et bras tendus: La contagion des symboles au temps du Front populaire," *Vingtième siècle* 11 (July-September

1986): 5-20.

Camparini, Aurelia. "Lotte e organizzazione delle donne dalla Liberazione agli anni Sessante," Aldo Agosti and Gian Mario Bravo, eds. *Storia del movimento operaio del socialismo e delle lotte sociali in Piemonte* (Bari: De Donato, 1980), vol. 4, pp. 555-99.

_____. *Questione femminile e Terza internazionale* (Bari: De Donato, 1978).

Caron, François. *Histoire économique de la France XIXe-XXe siècles* (Paris: Armand Colin, 1981).

Carr, E.H. *Twilight of the Comintern 1930-1935* (New York: Pantheon, 1982)

Castells, Manuel. *The City and the Grassroots* (Berkeley and Los Angeles: University of California Press, 1983).

Chambaz, Bernard. "L'implantation du Parti communiste française à Ivry," in Jacques Girault, ed. *Sur L'implantation du Parti communiste française dans l'entre deux guerres* (Paris: Editions sociales, 1977), pp. 147-77.

Chapman, Herrick. *State Capitalism and Working-Class Radicalism in the French Aircraft Industry* (Berkeley and Los Angeles: University of California Press, 1991).

Childers, Thomas. "The Social Language of Politics in Germany: The Sociology of Political Discourse in the Weimar Republic," *American Historical Review* 95:2 (April 1990): 331-58.

Clark, Martin. *Modern Italy, 1871-1982* (London: Longman, 1984).

Claudin, Fernando. *The Communist Movement: From Comintern to Cominform* (New York: Monthly Review Press, 1975).

Dear, Michael. "A Theory of the Local State,"' in Alan D. Burnett and Peter J. Taylor, eds. *Political Studies from Spatial Perspectives* (Chichester: Wiley, 1981), pp. 183-200.

De Grazia, Victoria. *The Culture of Consent: Mass Organization of Leisure in Fascist Italy* (Cambridge: Cambridge University Press, 1981).

_____. *How Fascism Ruled Women: Italy, 1922-1945* (Berkeley and Los Angeles: University of California Press, 1992).

Dellavalle, Claudio. "La classe operaia piedmontese nella guerra di Liberazione," in Aldo Agosti and Gian Mario Bravo, eds. *Storia del movimento operaio del socialismo e delle lotte sociali in Piemonte* (Bari: De Donato, 1980), pp. 305-62.

Delpla, François. "Les Communistes français et la sexualité (1932-1938)," *Mouvement social* 91 (1975): 121-52.

Depretto, Jean-Paul and Schweitzer, Sylvie V. *Le Communisme à l'Usine* (Roubaix: Edires, 1984).

Dorpalen, Andreas. "SPD und KPD in der Endphase der Weimarer

Republik," *Vierteljahreshefte für Zeitgeschichte* 31:1 (January 1983): 77-107.

Drachkovitch, Milorad M. and Lazitch, Branko, eds. *The Comintern: Historical Highlights* (New York: Praeger, 1966).

Ebbighausen, Rolf and Tiemann, Friedrich, eds. *Das Ende der Arbeiterbewegung in Deutschland? Ein Diskussionsband zum sechzigsten Geburtstag von Theo Pirker* (Opladen: Westdeutscher Verlag, 1984).

Eley, Geoff. "International Communism in the Heyday of Stalin," *New Left Review* 157 (May/June 1986): 90-100.

_____. "Labor History, Social History, Alltagsgeschichte: Experience, Culture, and the Politics of the Everyday--A New Direction for German Social History?," *Journal of Modern History* 61:2 (June 1989): 297-343.

Eley, Geoff and Suny, Ronald. "University of Michigan Project on International Communism," *International Labor and Working Class History* 30 (Fall 1986): 103-107.

Evans, Peter B.; Rueschemeyer, Dietrich; Skocpol, Theda, eds. *Bringing the State Back In* (Cambridge: Cambridge University Press, 1985).

Evans, Sara M. and Boyte, Harry C. *Free Spaces: The Sources of Democratic Change in America* (New York: Harper & Row, 1986).

Falter, Jürgen W. "Unemployment and the Radicalisation of the German Electorate, 1928-1933: An Aggregate Data Analysis with Special Emphasis on the Rise of National Socialism," in Peter D. Stachura, ed. *Unemployment and the Great Depression in Germany* (London: Macmillan, 1986), pp. 187-208.

Fischer, Conan. *The German Communists and the Rise of Nazism* (New York: St. Martin's Press, 1991).

Fischer, Ruth. *Stalin and German Communism* (1948; New Brunswick: Transaction Books, 1982).

Fohlen, Claude. "France 1920-1970," in Carlo M. Cipolla, ed. *The Fontana Economic History of Europe*, vol. 6: *Contemporary Economies*, part 1 (Sussex: Harvester Press, 1979), pp. 72-127.

Fourcaut, Annie. *Bobigny, Banlieue Rouge* (Paris: Èditions Ouvrières Presses de la Fondation Nationale des Sciences Politiques, 1986).

_____. "L'implantation du Parti communiste dans un groupe d'HBM: La Cité du Champ des Oiseaux à Bagneux (1932-1935)," in Jacques Girault, ed. *Sur L'implantation du Parti communiste française dans l'entre deux guerres* (Paris: Editions sociales, 1977), pp. 179-203.

_____. "La conquête d'une municipalité par le P.C.F. au moment du Front populaire: Les élections municipales de 1935 à Bagneux. Sur la validité d'une monographie communale," *Cahiers d'histoire de l'Institut Maurice Thorez* 19 (1976): 93-103.

Fridenson, Patrick. "Automobile Workers in France and Their Work, 1914-83," in Steven L. Kaplan and Cynthia J. Koepp, eds. *Work in France: Representations, Meaning, Organization, and Practice* (Ithaca: Cornell University Press, 1986), pp. 514-30.

Fülberth, Georg. *Die Beziehungen zwischen SPD und KPD in der Kommunalpolitik der Weimarer Periode 1918/19 bis 1933* (Cologne: Pahl-Rugenstein, 1985).

Galenson, Walter. "The Labour Force and Labour Problems in Europe 1920-1970," in Carlo M. Cipolla, ed. *The Fontana Economic History of Europe*, vol. 5 *The Twentieth Century*, part 1 (Sussex: Harvester Press, 1977), pp. 133-83.

Geschichte der VEB Leuna-Werke 'Walter Ulbricht' 1916 bis 1945 ed. Kreisleitung der SED des VEB Leuna-Werke 'Walter Ulbricht' (Leuna, 1989).

Ghini, Celso. "Gli iscritti al partito e alla FGCI 1943/1979," in Massimo Illardi and Aris Accornero, eds. *Il Partito comunista italiano: Struttura e storia dell'organizzazione 1921/1979*, Fondazione Giangiacomo Feltrinelli, *Annali* 21 (1981): 227-92.

Gianotti, Renzo. *Lotte e organizzazioni di classe alla FIAT (1948-1970)* (Bari: De Donato, 1970).

Giddens, Anthony. *Central Problems in Social Theory: Action, Structure and Contradiction in Social Analysis* (Berkeley and Los Angeles: University of California Press, 1979).

_____. *The Constitution of Society: Outline of the Theory of Structuration* (Berkeley and Los Angeles: University of California Press, 1984).

Gillet, Marcel. "L'évolution du Parti communiste de 1921 à 1934 dan la région Nord-Pas-de-Calais," *Revue du Nord* 221 (April-June 1974): 233-38.

Ginsborg, Paul. "The Communist Party and the Agrarian Question in Southern Italy, 1943-48," *History Workshop* 17 (Spring 1984): 81-101.

_____. *A History of Contemporary Italy: Society and Politics 1943-1988* (London: Penguin Books, 1990).

Girault, Jacques, ed. *Sur L'implantation du Parti communiste française dans l'entre deux guerres* (Paris: Editions sociales, 1977).

Gobetti, Ada Marchesini. "Perchè erano tante nella Resistenza," *Rinascita* 3 (March 1961): 245-51.

Gorz, André. *Farewell to the Working Class: An Essay on Post-Industrial Socialism* (London, 1982).

Gout, Étienne; Juvigny, Pierre; Mousel, Michel. "La Politique sociale du Front populaire," in Pierre Renouvin and Réné Rémond, eds. *Léon Blum: Chef de Gouvernement 1936-1937*, 2nd ed. (Paris: Presses de la Fondation Nationale des Sciences Politiques, 1981), pp. 241-76.

Graham, Helen and Preston, Paul. "The Popular Front and the Struggle against Fascism," in Graham and Preston, eds. *The Popular Front in Europe* (New York: St. Martin's Press, 1987), pp. 1-19.

Gramsci, Antonio. *Selections from the Prison Notebooks*, ed. Quintin Hoare and Geoffrey Nowell Smith (New York: International Publishers, 1971).

Gray, Lawrence. "From Gramsci to Togliatti: The *Partito Nuovo* and the Mass Basis of Italian Communism," in Simon Serfaty and Lawrence Gray, eds. *The Italian Communist Party: Yesterday, Today, and Tomorrow* (Westport: Greenwood Press, 1980), pp. 21-35.

Grossmann, Atina. "Abortion and Economic Crisis: The 1931 Campaign Against Paragraph 218," in Renate Bridenthal, Atina Grossmann, and Marion Kaplan, eds. *When Biology Became Destiny: Women in Weimar and Nazi Germany* (New York: Monthly Review Press, 1984), pp. 66-86.

Gruber, Helmut. *Soviet Russia Masters the Comintern: International Communism in the Era of Stalin's Ascendancy* (New York: Anchor Books, 1974).

Gualerni, Gualberto. *Industria e fascismo: Per una interpretazione dello sviluppo economico italiano tra le due guerre* (Milan: Vita e Pensiero, 1976).

Hainsworth, Raymond. "Les Grèves du Front populaire de mai et juin 1936: Une nouvelle analyse fondée sur l'étude de ces grèves dans le bassin houiller du Nord et du Pas-de-Calais," *Mouvement social* 96 (1976): 3-30.

Hardy-Hémery, Odette. "Rationalisation technique et rationalisation du travail à la Compagnie des Mines d'Anzin," *Mouvement social* 72 (1970): 3-48.

Harvey, David. *The Condition of Postmodernity: An Enquiry into the Origins of Cultural Change* (Oxford: Basil Blackwell, 1989).

Harvey, David. *Consciousness and the Urban Experience: Studies in the History and Theory of Capitalist Urbanization* (Baltimore: Johns Hopkins University Press, 1985).

Haslam, Jonathan. "The Comintern and the Origins of the Popular Front, 1934-1935," *Historical Journal* 25:3 (September 1979): 673-91.

Heer-Kleinert, Lore. *Die Gewerkschaftspolitik der KPD in der Weimarer Republik* (Frankfurt a.M: Campus Verlag, 1983).

Hellman, Judith Adler. *Journeys among Women: Feminism in Five Italian Cities* (New York: Oxford University Press, 1987).

Herlemann, Beatrix. *Kommunalpolitik der KPD im Ruhrgebiet 1924-1933* (Wuppertal: Peter Hammer Verlag, 1977).

Humbert-Droz, Jules. *Archives de Jules Humbert-Droz*, 3 vols., ed. Institute for Social History (Dordrecht: D. Reidel, 1970).

_____. *De Lénine à Staline: Dix Ans au Service de l'Internationale communiste 1921-1931. Memoires de Jules Humbert-Droz*, vol. 2 (Neuchâtel: Editions de la Baconnière, 1971).

Illardi, Massimo and Accornero, Aris, eds. *Il Partito comunista italiano: Struttura e storia dell'organizzazione 1921/1979*, Fondazione Giangiacomo Feltrinelli, *Annali* 21 (1981).

Jackson, Julian. *The Politics of Depression in France, 1932-1936* (Cambridge: Cambridge University Press, 1985).

_____. *The Popular Front in France: Defending Democracy, 1934-1938* (Cambridge: Cambridge University Press, 1988).

Jacques, Martin and Mulhern, Francis, eds. *The Forward March of Labour Halted?* (London: Verso, 1982).

Jodice, Yedid. "L'organizzazione del 'partito nuovo': Il PCI torinese nel 1945-56," in Aldo Agosti and Gian Mario Bravo, eds. *Storia del movimento operaio del socialismo e delle lotte sociali in Piemonte* (Bari: De Donato, 1980), pp. 71-121.

Judt, Tony. "Une historiographie pas comme les autres: The French Communists and their History," *European Studies Review* 12:4 (October 1982): 445-78.

_____. *Marxism and the French Left: Studies in Labour and Politics in France, 1830-1981* (Oxford: Clarendon Press, 1986).

_____. "'The Spreading Notion of the Town': Some Recent Writings on French and Italian Communism," *Historical Journal* 28:4 (December 1985): 1011-1021.

Kaasch, Wienand. "Die soziale Struktur der KPD," *Kommunistische Internationale* 9:19 (1928): 1050-64.

Kämpfendes Leuna: Die Geschichte des Kampfes der Leuna Arbeiter, Teil I, 1. Halbband (1916-1933) (Berlin: Verlag Tribüne, 1961).

Kirby, Andrew. "A Public City: Concepts of Space and the Local State," *Urban Geography* 4:3 (1983): 191-202.

_____. "State, Local State, Context, and Spatiality: A Reappraisal of State Theory," in James A. Caporaso, ed. *The Elusive State: International and Comparative Perspectives* (London: Sage, 1989), pp. 204-26.

_____. "Time, Space and Collective Action: Political Space/Political Geography," (ms., 1989).

Koenker, Diane P.; Rosenberg, William G.; Suny, Ronald Grigor, eds. *Party, State, and Society in the Russian Civil War:*

Explorations in Social History (Bloomington: Indiana University Press, 1989).

Kolakowski, Leszek. *Main Currents of Marxism*, vol. 2: *The Golden Age* (Oxford: Oxford University Press, 1978).

Kontos, Silvia. *Die Partei kämpft wie ein Mann: Frauenpolitik der KPD in der Weimarer Republik* (Frankfurt a. M.: Verlag Roter Stern, 1979).

Kriegel, Annie. *Les Communistes français dans leur premier demi siècle 1920-1970*, 2nd ed. (Paris: Editions du Seuil, 1985).

_____. "Les Communistes français et la question du pouvoir (1920-1939)," *Annales: économies, sociétés, civilisations* 21:6 (November-December 1966): 1245-58

_____. "Léon Blum et le Parti communiste," in Pierre Renouvin and Réné Rémond, eds. *Léon Blum: Chef de Gouvernement 1936-1937*, 2nd ed. (Paris: Presses de la Fondation Nationale des Sciences Politiques, 1981), pp. 125-35.

_____. *Aux Origines du communisme français 1914-1920*, 2 vols. (Paris: Mouton, 1964).

Kuisel, Richard F. *Capitalism and the State in Modern France: Renovation and Economic Management in the Twentieth Century* (Cambridge: Cambridge University Press, 1981).

LaFrancesca, Salvatore. *La politica economia del fascismo*, (1972; Rome: Laterza, 1976).

Laclau, Ernesto. *New Reflections on the Revolution of Our Time* (London: Verso, 1990).

Laclau, Ernesto and Mouffe, Chantal. *Hegemony and Socialist Strategy: Towards a Radical Democratic Politics* (London: Verso, 1985).

Lange, Peter; Ross, George; Vannicelli, Maurizio. *Unions, Change and Crisis: French and Italian Union Strategy and the Political Economy, 1945-1980* (London: George Allen & Unwin, 1982).

Lanzardo, Liliana. "I Consigli di gestione nella strategia della collaborazione," in Aris Accornero, ed. *Problemi del movimento sindacale in Italia 1943-1973*, Fondazione Giangiacomo Feltrinelli, *Annali* 16 (1974-1975): 325-65.

Lavau, Georges. "Le Parti communiste dans le système politique français," in *Le Communisme en France*, Cahiers de la Fondation Nationale des Sciences Politiques no. 175 (Paris: Armand Colin, 1969), pp. 7-65.

Luxemburg, Rosa. *Rosa Luxemburg Speaks*, ed. Mary-Alice Waters (New York: Pathfinder Press, 1970).

_____. *Gesammelte Werke*, vol. 2-4, ed. Institut für Marxismus-Leninismus beim ZK der SED (Berlin: Dietz Verlag, 1972-74).

Lyttelton, Adrian. *The Seizure of Power: Fascism in Italy, 1919-1929*

(London: Weidenfeld and Nicolson, 1973).

Mafai, Miriam. *L'apprendistato della politica: Le donne italiane nel dopoguerra* (Rome: Riuniti, 1979).

Maier, Charles S. "The Economics of Fascism and Nazism," in Maier, *In Search of Stability: Explorations in Historical Political Economy* (Cambridge: Cambridge University Press, 1987), pp. 70-120.

Mancini, Federico. "The Theoretical Roots of Italian Communism: Worker Democracy and Political Party in Gramsci's Thinking," in Simon Serfaty and Lawrence Gray, eds. *The Italian Communist Party: Yesterday, Today, and Tomorrow* (Westport: Greenwood Press, 1980), pp. 3-20.

Martelli, Roger. "Une introduction à l'année 1934: Le PCF, l'Internationale et la France," *Cahiers d'histoire de l'Institut Maurice Thorez* 18 (1984): 5-23.

Mason, Tim. "Gli scioperi di Torino del marzo 1943," in Francesca Ferratini Tosi, et. al., eds. *L'Italia nella seconda guerra mondiale e nella Resistenza* (Milan: Franco Angeli Libri, 1988), pp. 399-422.

_____. "Women in Germany, 1925-1940: Family, Welfare and Work," 2 parts *History Workshop* 1 (1978): 74-111 and 2 (1978): 5-32.

Massola, Umbertto. "Gli scioperi del '43," in Ernesto Ragionieri, ed. *I comunisti a Torino 1919-1972: Lezioni e testimonianze* (Rome: Riuniti, 1974), pp. 135-39.

Miliband, Ralph. *The State in Capitalist Society* (New York: Basic Books, 1969).

Mitchell, B.R. "Statistical Appendix," in Carlo M. Cipolla, ed. *The Fontana Economic History of Europe*, vol. 6: *Contemporary Economies*, part 2 (Sussex: Harvester Press, 1979), pp. 625-755.

Mora, Alba. "Per una storia dell'associazionismo femminile a Parma: GDD e UDI tra emancipazione e tradizione (1943-1946)," in Fiorenzo Sicuri, ed. *Comunisti a Parma: Atti del convegno tenutosi a Parma il 7 Novembre 1981* (Parma: STEP Cooperativa, 1986), pp. 299-348.

Moutet, Aimée. "La Rationalisation dans les mines du Nord à l'épreuve du Front populaire: Etude d'après les sources imprimées," *Mouvement social* 135 (April-June 1986): 63-99.

Müller, Werner. *Lohnkampf, Massenstreik, Sowjetmacht: Ziele und Grenzen der "Revolutionären Gewerkschafts-Opposition" (RGO) in Deutschland 1928 bis 1933* (Cologne: Bund-Verlag, 1988).

Natta, Alessandro. "La Resistenza e la formazione del 'partito nuovo,'" in Paolo Spriano, et. al, *Problemi di storia del Partito comunista italiano* (Rome: Editori Riuniti, 1971), pp. 57-83.

Nettl, J.P. "The State as a Conceptual Variable," *World Politics* 20:4 (July 1968): 559-92.

_____. *Rosa Luxemburg*, abridged ed. (Oxford: Oxford University Press, 1969).

Nolan, Mary. "'Housework made Easy': The Taylorized Housewife in Weimar Germany's Rationalized Economy," *Feminist Studies* 16:3 (Fall 1990): 549-73.

Offe, Claus. "Challenging the Boundaries. of Institutional Politics: Social Movements since the 1960s," in Charles S. Maier, *Changing Boundaries of the Political: Essays on the Evolving Balance between the State and Society, Public and Private in Europe* (Cambridge: Cambridge University Press, 1987), pp. 63-105.

Peukert, Detlev. "The Lost Generation: Youth Unemployment and the End of the Weimar Republic," in Richard J. Evans and Dick Geary, eds. *The German Unemployed: Experiences and Consequences of Mass Unemployment from the Weimar Republic to the Third Reich* (London: Croom Helm, 1987), pp. 261-80.

Pjatnitzki, O. "Die Errungenschaften, die Mängel und die nächsten Aufgaben der Organisationsarbeit der KI-Sektionen," *Kommunistische Internationale* 8:17 (April 1927): 820-30; 8:18 (May 1927): 879-91; 8:19 (May 1927): 928-33.

Poulantzas, Nicos. *Political Power and Social Classes* (London: NLB & S&W, 1973).

Pred, Allan. *Place, Practice and Structure: Social and Spatial Transformation in Southern Sweden, 1750-1850* (Totowa, New Jersey: Barnes & Noble Books, 1986).

Prost, Antoine. "Le Climat social," in Réné Rémond and Janine Bourdin, eds. *Edouard Daladier, Chef du Gouvernement* (Paris: Presses de la Fondation Nationale des Sciences Politiques, 1977), pp. 99-111.

_____. "Les Grèves de Juin 1936: Essai d'interprétation," in Pierre Renouvin and Réné Rémond, eds. *Léon Blum: Chef de Gouvernement 1936-1937*, 2nd ed. (Paris: Presses de la Fondation Nationale des Sciences Politiques, 1981), pp. 69-87.

Ragionieri, Ernesto. "Il giudizio sul fascismo. La lotta contro il fascismo. I rapporti con l'Internazionale comunista," in Paolo Spriano, et. al, *Problemi di storia del Partito comunista italiano* (Rome: Editori Riuniti, 1971), pp. 33-55.

_____. "Il PCI nella Resistenza: La nascita del 'partito nuovo,'" *Studi Storici* 10:1 (January-March 1969): 83-113.

Regards, Paris (1934 to 1938).

Rémond, Réné and Bourdin, Janine, eds. *Edouard Daladier, Chef du Gouvernement* (Paris: Presses de la Fondation Nationale des

Sciences Politiques, 1977).

_____. *La France et les Français en 1938-1939* (Paris: Presses de la Fondation Nationale des Science Politiques, 1978).

Renouvin, Pierre and Rémond, Réné, eds. *Léon Blum: Chef de Gouvernement 1936-1937*, 2nd ed. (Paris: Presses de la Fondation Nationale des Sciences Politiques, 1981).

Reynolds, Siân. "Women, Men and the 1936 Strikes in France," in Martin S. Alexander and Helen Graham, eds. *The French and Spanish Popular Fronts: Comparative Perspectives* (Cambridge: Cambridge University Press, 1989), pp. 185-200.

Rioux, Jean-Pierre. "La conciliation et l'arbitrage obligatoire des conflits du travail," in Réné Rémond and Janine Bourdin, eds. *Edouard Daladier, Chef du Gouvernement* (Paris: Presses de la Fondation Nationale des Sciences Politiques, 1977), pp. 112-28.

Robert, Jean-Louis. "Women and Work in France during the First World War," in Richard Wall and Jay Winter, eds. *The Upheaval of War: Family, Work and Welfare in Europe, 1914-1918* (Cambridge: Cambridge University Press, 1989), pp. 251-66.

Robrieux, Philippe. *Histoire intérieure du Parti communiste*, vol. 1: *1920-1945* (Paris: Fayard, 1980).

Romeo, Rosario. *Breve storia de la grande industria in italia 1861-1961* (1961; Bologna: Cappelli Editore, 1980).

Rosenhaft, Eve. *Beating the Fascists? The German Communists and Political Violence, 1929-1933* (Cambridge: Cambridge University Press, 1983).

_____. "Working-Class Life and Working-Class Politics: Communists, Nazis and the State in the Battle for the Streets, Berlin 1928-1932," in Richard Bessel and E.J. Feuchtwanger, eds. *Social Change and Political Development in Weimar Germany* (London: Croom Helm, 1981), pp. 207-40.

Ross, George. *Workers and Communists in France: From Popular Front to Eurocommunism* (Berkeley and Los Angeles: University of California Press, 1982).

Rossiter, Adrian. "The Blum Government, the Conseil National Économique and Economic Policy," in Martin S. Alexander and Helen Graham, eds. *The French and Spanish Popular Fronts: Comparative Perspectives* (Cambridge: Cambridge University Press, 1989), pp. 156-70.

_____. "Popular Front Economic Policy and the Matignon Negotiations," *Historical Journal* 30:3 (September 1987): 663-84.

Salvati, B. "The Rebirth of Italian Trade Unionism, 1943-54," in S.J. Woolf, ed. *The Rebirth of Italy, 1943-50* (London: Longman, 1972).

Santore, John. "The Comintern's United Front Initiative of May

1934: French or Soviet Inspiration?" *Canadian Journal of History* 16 (December 1981): 405-23.

Sassoon, Donald. *The Strategy of the Italian Communist Party: From the Resistance to the Historic Compromise* (New York: St. Martin's Press, 1981).

Sauvy, Alfred. *Histoire économique de la France entre les deux guerres*, vol. 2 (Paris: Ed. Economica, 1984).

Schneider, William H. "The Eugenics Movement in France, 1890-1940," in Mark B. Adams, ed. *The Wellborn Science: Eugenics in Germany, France, Brazil, and Russia* (New York: Oxford University Press, 1990), pp. 69-109.

Schöck, Eva Cornelia. *Arbeitslosigkeit und Rationalisierung: Die Lage der Arbeiter und die kommunistische Gewerkschaftspolitik 1920-1928* (Frankfurt a.M.: Campus Verlag, 1977).

Schuster, Kurt G.P. *Der Rote Frontkämpferbund 1924-1929: Beiträge zur Geschichte und Organisationsstruktur eines politischen Kampfbundes* (Düsseldorf: Droste Verlag, 1975).

Sheppard, Eric and Barnes, Trevor J. *The Capitalist Space Economy: Geographical Analysis after Ricardo, Marx and Sfarra* (London: Unwin Hyman, 1990).

Sivini, Giordano. "Le Parti communiste: Struture et fonctionnement," in *Sociologie du communisme en Italie*, Cahiers de la Fondation Nationale des Sciences Politiques no. 194 (Paris: Armand Colin, 1974), pp. 55-141.

Spano, Nadia and Camarlinghi, Fiamma. *La questione femminile nella politica del PCI 1921-1963* (Rome: Ed. Donne e Politica, 1972).

Spriano, Paolo. *Storia del Partito comunista italiano*, 5 vols. (Turin: Einaudi, 1967-75).

Spriano, Paolo et. al. *Problemi di storia del Partito comunista italiano* (Rome: Editori Riuniti, 1971).

Sewell, William H., Jr. "A Theory of Structure: Duality, Agency, and Transformation," *American Journal of Sociology* 98:1 (July 1992): 1-29.

Stachura, Peter D. *The Weimar Republic and the Younger Proletariat: An Economic and Social Analysis* (New York: St. Martin's Press, 1989).

Stovall, Tyler. "'Friends, Neighbors, and Communists': Community Formation in Suburban Paris during the early Twentieth Century," *Journal of Social History* 22:2 (Winter 1988): 237-54.

_____. "French Communism and Suburban Development: The Rise of the Paris Red Belt," *Journal of Contemporary History* 24:3 (July 1989): 437-60.

_____. *The Rise of the Paris Red Belt* (Berkeley and Los Angeles: University of California Press, 1990).

Sullerot, Evelyne. "Condition de la femme," in Albert Sauvy, *Histoire économique de la France entre les deux guerres*, vol. 3 (Paris: Editions Economica, 1984), pp. 195ff.

Tarrow, Sidney. *Democracy and Disorder: Protest and Politics in Italy, 1965-1975* (Oxford: Clarendon Press, 1989).

_____. "Le Parti communiste e la société italienne," in *Sociologie du communisme en Italie*, Cahiers de la Fondation Nationale des Sciences Politiques no. 194 (Paris: Armand Colin, 1974), pp. 1-53.

_____. *Peasant Communism in Southern Italy* (New Haven: Yale University Press, 1967).

_____. *Struggle, Politics, and Reform: Collective Action, Social Movements, and Cycles of Protest*, Cornell Studies in International Affairs: Western Societies Program Occasional Paper No. 21 (Ithaca: Cornell University Center for International Studies, 1989).

Tartakowsky, Danielle. "Le P.C.F. et les femmes (1926)," *Cahiers d'histoire de l'Institut Maurice Thorez* 14 (1975): 194-225.

Tasca, Angelo. Archives, Istituto Giangiacomo Feltrinelli, *Annali* 11 (1966) and 14 (1969).

Tilly, Charle. "Warmaking as Statemaking," in Peter B. Evans, Dietrich Rueschemeyer, and Theda Skocpol, eds. *Bringing the State Back In* (Cambridge: Cambridge University Press, 1985), pp. 169-91.

Togliatti, Palmiro. *L'emancipazione femminile* (Rome: Editori Riuniti, 1965).

_____. *Opere*, vol. 4, part 1, ed. Franco Andreucci and Paolo Spriano (Rome: Riuniti, 1979).

Toniolo, Gianni. *L'Economia dell'italia fascista* (Rome: Editori Laterza, 1980).

Touchard, Jean and Bodin, Louis. "L'État de l'opinion au début de l'année 1936," in Pierre Renouvin and Réné Rémond, eds. *Léon Blum: Chef de Gouvernement 1936-1937*, 2nd ed. (Paris: Presses de la Fondation Nationale des Sciences Politiques, 1981), pp. 49-68.

Travis, D.J. "Communism in Modena: The Provincial Origins of the Partito comunista italiano (1943-1945)," *Historical Journal* 29:4 (December 1986): 875-95.

Turone, Sergio. *Storia del sindacato in Italia (1943-1969): Dalla Resistenza all' "autunno caldo"* (Rome: Laterza, 1975).

l'Unità, Rome (1945-1948).

Vassart, Célie and Vassart, Albert. "The Moscow Origins of the French 'Popular Front,'" in Milorad M. Drachkovitch and Branko Lazitch, eds. *The Comintern: Historical Highlights* (New York: Praeger, 1966), pp. 234-52.

Vassart, Albert. Memoirs (typescript, Hoover Institution Archives).

Weber, Hermann. *Aufbau und Fall einer Diktatur: Kritischen Beiträge zur Geschichte der DDR* (Cologne: Bund-Verlag, 1991).

_____, ed. *Der Gründungsparteitag der KPD: Protokoll und Materialien* (Frankfurt a.M.: Europäische Verslagsanstalt, 1969).

_____. *Kommunistische Bewegung und realsozialistischer Staat: Beiträge zum deutschen und internationalen Kommunismus. Hermann Weber zum 60. Geburtstag*, ed. Werner Müller (Cologne: Bund-Verlag, 1988).

_____. *Die Wandlung des deutschen Kommunismus: Die Stalinisierung der KPD in der Weimarer Republik*, 2 vols. (Frankfurt a.M.: Europäische Verlagsanstalt, 1969).

Weitz, Eric D. "Bukharin and 'Bukharinism' in the Comintern, 1919-1929," in Nicholas N. Kozlov and Eric D. Weitz, eds. *Nikolai Ivanovich Bukharin: A Centenary Appraisal* (New York: Praeger, 1990), pp. 59-91.

_____. "State Power, Class Fragmentation, and the Shaping of German Communist Politics, 1890-1933," *Journal of Modern History* 62:2 (June 1990): 279-93.

Wellner, G. "Industriearbeiterinnen in der Weimarer Republik: Arbeitsmarkt, Arbeit und Privatleben 1919-1933," *Geschichte und Gesellschaft* 7 (1981): 534-54.

Winkler, Heinrich August. *Der Schein der Normalität: Arbeiter und Arbeiterbewegung in der Weimarer Republik 1924 bis 1930* (Berlin: Dietz, 1985).

_____. *Von der Revolution zur Stabilisierung: Arbeiter und Arbeiterbewegung in der Weimarer Republik 1918 bis 1924* (Berlin: Dietz, 1984).

_____. *Der Weg in die Katastrophe: Arbeiter und Arbeiterbewegung in der Weimarer Republik 1930 bis 1933* (Berlin: Dietz, 1987).

Wollenberg, Erich. Memoirs (typescript, Hoover Institution Archives).

Yannakakis, M.I. "Le P.C.F. dans la région du Nord (1920-1936)," *Revue du Nord* 221 (April-June 1974): 239-45.

Zetkin, Clara. "Richtlinien für die Kommunistische Frauenbewegung," *Kommunistische Internationale* 3:15 (1921): 530-55.

_____. *Um Rosa Luxemburgs Stellung zur russischen Revolution* (Hamburg: Verlag Carl Hoym Nachf., 1922).